My Work among the Florida Seminoles

by *James Lafayette Glenn*

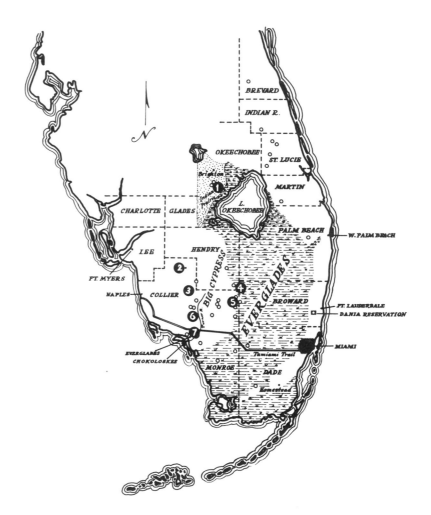

Location of Seminole Camps
circa 1930

○ Seminole camps ● Camps mentioned in text
● Towns

DRAWN BY H.A. SCHUBERT (AFTER NASH)

1. Billie Stewart's
2. Immokalee
3. Josie Billy's
4. Guava Camp
5. Californee
6. Johnny Buster's
7. Charlie Tigertail's

My Work among the Florida Seminoles

by *James Lafayette Glenn*

EDITED AND WITH AN INTRODUCTION
BY HARRY A. KERSEY, JR.

Published with the support of
Fort Lauderdale Historical Society, Inc.

A University of Central Florida Book

UNIVERSITY PRESSES OF FLORIDA
Orlando

Printed in the United States of America
The paper in this book meets the guidelines for
permanence and durability of the committee on
Production Guidelines for Book Longevity of the
Council on Library Resources.

University Presses of Florida is the central
agency for scholarly publishing of the State of
Florida's university system. Its offices are located at 15 NW 15th Street, Gainesville, FL
32603. Works published by University Presses of
Florida are evaluated and selected for publication
by a faculty editorial committee of any one of
Florida's nine public universities: Florida A&M
University (Tallahassee), Florida Atlantic Uni-
versity (Boca Raton), Florida International Uni-
versity (Miami), Florida State University (Talla-
hassee), University of Central Florida (Orlando),
University of Florida (Gainesville), University of
North Florida (Jacksonville), University of South
Florida (Tampa), University of West Florida
(Pensacola).

Library of Congress Cataloging in Publication Data

Glenn, James Lafayette.
   My work among the Florida Seminoles.

"A University of Central Florida book."
Includes index.
   1. Seminole Indians. 2. Seminole Indians—Government relations. 3. Glenn, James Lafayette. 4. Indian
agents—Florida—Biography. I. Kersey, Harry A.,
1935 - . II. Title.
E99.S28G57   975.9'00497   81-19794
ISBN 0-8130-0717-8   AACR2

Contents

Foreword

by SAMUEL PROCTOR

"If I could have the voice of a god for just one statement I would use it to say that all of this pageantry, this difference between them and us, is secondary. Basically and fundamentally we and they are members of one and the same human family." This was the belief and philosophy of life of James L. Glenn, who was appointed Special Commissioner to the Florida Seminoles in 1931. Glenn was appalled at how the Indians were being treated by the bureaucracy on both the national and state level. Every Indian, he insisted, was "a just and rightful member of the American citizenship" and not a stepchild. In this long letter to his niece, Glenn has detailed his life and his activities fighting for the rights of these Florida Indians.

Glenn resented the shoddy tourist shows where Indians were displayed as though they were circus curiosities. He disapproved of the bootleggers who made whiskey available to the Indians. These peddlers of "low bush lightning" were the "muck and mire that sucked under the character of both the individual Indian and the whole social body of the tribe." Glenn criticized the "professionalized uplifter" who wanted to change the Indian lifestyle, by force if necessary. And he abhorred the "hobbiest uplifter," who, in a superficial way, proclaimed the pageantry of Indian life and culture. He referred to a Miami lady with "wealth and time to waste," who, dressed in Seminole garments, needed little encouragement to deliver "a half-baked harangue about letting the Indian be an Indian." These people, Glenn felt, hindered his achieving his goals of raising the Seminole standard of living, increasing health facilities, making land and educational opportunities more available, improving job opportunities, and protecting the Indians against all who wanted to exploit and take advantage of them.

Glenn has produced a valuable memoir describing the day-to-day activities of a handful of Indians during an important transitional period. They had been living for many generations isolated for the most part from white people. Poor and illiterate, they seemed content. They provided for their own food, recreation, social, and religious needs. Occasionally they left their camps to exchange animal pelts and skins and egret plumes for supplies at the trading post. These meetings were their only contacts with the outside world. Then things began to change, and very rapidly. Attracted by the land boom of the 1920s, large numbers of white people moved into south Florida. Speculators and developers looked with greedy eyes on property throughout the area, including Indian homesites and hunting grounds, which they wanted to turn into urban centers. The major problem was the Indians themselves, because many insisted upon acting and looking "different" from their white neighbors. The Indians could not halt the encroachments, upon either their land or their way of life. It was Commissioner Glenn's responsibility, as he saw it, to try to protect the Indians.

The Florida Seminole is not only one of the most conservative of American Indian groups; it is also one about which relatively little is known. The Glenn memoir and its photographs provide information about the Seminoles during the 1930s that is nowhere else available. Other manuscripts may be hidden away in family records or in local historical society archives, but the chances of such material being made available to the scholarly community in published form are not good. Costs prohibit their private printing, and they are not the kind of material that has appeal for commercial publishers. University presses have accepted the special responsibility for publishing this kind of historical source material when they can, and in this case the assistance of the Fort Lauderdale Historical Society and the University of Central Florida editorial committee has also been necessary to make this book possible. James L. Glenn's memoir is a boon to all persons interested not only in the Florida Seminoles but also in the plight of any minority group whose existence is threatened by forces over which it has little or no control.

Samuel Proctor

Introduction

by HARRY A. KERSEY, JR.

In 1930, as the nation poised on the brink of the abyss of the Great Depression, the federal Indian Service sent an official to conduct a comprehensive survey of the conditions among the Seminole Indians in Florida, a state already experiencing economic hardships. His name was Roy Nash, and his landmark report was the first attempt to assess the Florida Indians in over half a century. Nash found an Indian population that was already a poverty stricken and dispossessed minority in their own land. The drainage of the Everglades and ensuing collapse of the Seminole's hunting and trapping economy, coupled with rapid growth of the white population in south Florida, had forced the Indians into a marginal existence well in advance of the coming national economic disaster.

The Seminoles still occupied the territory in which they had been found prior to the turn of the century. In the region of the Everglades and the Big Cypress Swamp, the Mikasuki-speaking Seminoles lived in widely scattered camps of extended families where they carried on subsistence farming supplemented by hunting, fishing, and the raising of some livestock. To the north, in the pine and palmetto woods around Lake Okeechobee, the Cow Creek band of Seminoles made their camps. They too were subsistence farmers who tended some livestock, and often lived on the land of whites for whom they worked. The East Coast camps were the first to be impacted by the burgeoning non-Indian population, and by 1930 most of those Seminole families were crowded into the newly opened Dania Reservation west of Fort Lauderdale. Still others moved to tourist camps in the Miami area or squatted along the Tamiami Trail, eking out a meager existence by selling souvenirs to tourists.

All of these groups were impoverished, suffered from general bad health and poor nutrition, and were abused by their non-Indian neighbors. Nash felt that a strong effort was necessary to get as many Seminoles as possible onto federal trust land where their needs could be met. Since 1913 the Seminoles had been served by Agent L. A. Spencer, whose long years of service were now drawing to a close. When Spencer died while pursuing his duties in the Big Cypress region, Nash believed that a suitable replacement was to be found in the minister of the church at Everglades City, James L. Glenn.

A thirty-nine-year-old Texan, Glenn was a graduate of both Trinity University and Lane Theological Seminary in Ohio. Although he had long been interested in the American Indian tribes and had studied their history, Glenn had not had direct contact with any of the tribes in his native Southwest. After holding positions in Ohio and Oklahoma, Glenn and his wife arrived at Everglades City in 1924; he had accepted a post in the community church at the frontier town that had become a governmental and commercial center of the newly formed Collier County. The young minister's family soon became a fixture of the local society. Two of the Glenn children were born during their sojourn there. In addition to his preaching and other civic activities, Glenn also served briefly as editor of the local newspaper. Certainly the Reverend Mr. Glenn was a close associate of D. Graham Copeland, chief engineer and director of Collier Corporation operations in Everglades City. Apparently the work of the young minister had not gone unnoticed by Barron Collier, the millionaire developer who was opening up the southwestern frontier of the state. Thus when it was thought that Captain Spencer was going to resign as Seminole Agent in 1928, Collier wrote to support Glenn for the position. This effort proved to be premature, but when Spencer died two years later, the Collier interests again urged Glenn's selection.

Glenn had come to know the Seminoles, for the families who lived at nearby Turner River had frequented Everglades City; he also befriended their head men. Through this contact he initiated an "open air school" at the camp and went there several times a month to teach the children. He was greatly concerned with the welfare of the Seminoles, and he feared that the cross-state Tamiami Trail, which opened in 1928, would be a disruptive influence on their culture. Roy Nash agreed that the minister was a good choice to replace Spencer and nominated him for the post. After a brief meeting with the commissioner of Indian Affairs in Washington, Glenn was appointed special commissioner to the Seminoles of Florida in 1931.

Agent Glenn's efforts during his five years in this position might be considered in four major categories. His initial concern was the rehabilitation of the Indian community at the Dania Reservation, where the U.S. Indian Service headquarters was located. This meant the upgrading of Indian housing, improvement of health facilities and the government school, as well as the expansion of employment opportunities. During the depths of the Great Depression various New Deal programs such as the Civil Works Administration and the Indian Emergency Conservation Work operated at Dania Reservation, and Seminoles from throughout the state came there seeking work. This expanded population placed a strain on the physical facilities and created a high degree of social stress, which Agent Glenn was constantly mediating.

Because the bulk of the Seminole population lived in widely dispersed camps a great distance from the Dania Reservation, Glenn spent much of his time traveling thousands of miles each year to maintain contact with this constituency. Thus the second phase of his work centered around bringing relief supplies to indigent or incapacitated Indians, getting the sick and injured to doctors or hospitals, and protecting Seminole legal rights where they were jeopardized by the actions of local communities. A third element of Agent Glenn's work was his persistent but futile struggle to thwart the numerous bootleggers who supplied illicit whiskey to the Seminole camps, thereby causing untold suffering. Glenn found another source of Indian degradation to be the shoddy "tourist camps" in which Seminoles were displayed and demeaned for profit. Much of his time was spent in monitoring these camps—some of which were run by Indians on the Tamiami Trail—to assure that the inhabitants were at least being dealt with in a humane manner.

In the long run, perhaps the most important task that Glenn undertook as agent was securing land for the Seminoles. He was primarily interested in acquiring large tracts of good grazing land upon which to establish a Seminole cattle industry as a basis for their future economic and social renascence. By the end of his tenure the first elements of the Brighton Reservation had been secured and a starter herd of beef cattle made available to the tribe. This was to be the capstone of Glenn's work among the Seminoles.

Glenn's zealous pursuit of these objectives often brought him into conflict with vested interests both in Florida and in the nation's capital. Many individuals and groups in the state deeply involved with the Seminoles did not believe that the U.S. Indian Service was doing enough for the tribe, and there was a certain degree of personal animosity toward Glenn. Some groups had developed their own agenda for Seminole rehabilitation, which did not coincide with official government efforts. Obviously, individuals like the tourist camp operators and the whiskey vendors, who made money from their dealings with the Indians, felt that there was too much federal intervention. Then, too, there appears to have been a certain ambivalence in Indian attitudes toward Agent Glenn and the government programs that he represented. In 1934 the *Miami News* ran a series of exposé articles depicting the federal efforts to assist the Seminoles as a failure and portraying

Glenn in less than flattering terms. Actually, Glenn appears to have conscientiously carried out his duties as well as possible given the conditions of the period.

This assault by the daily press, as well as individual complaints to Washington, did not fall on deaf ears in the U.S. Indian Service. Glenn had been an annoyance to those bureaucrats by his persistent efforts to secure more land for the Seminoles and by his criticism of what he considered to be unwarranted obstruction by various federal agencies and departments within the Indian Service. Moreover, as a holdover appointee of the Hoover administration, he was suspect among the New Dealers surrounding the new Commissioner of Indian Affairs, John Collier. By 1935 all of these forces had combined to make Glenn highly expendable, and he was removed as special commissioner to the Florida Seminoles. He stayed on as financial clerk until early 1936, when he left government service to return to the ministry.

Glenn did meet with Commissioner Collier in Washington and was given an opportunity to present his side of the story, but he opted not to defend his record of service. It is difficult to judge whether Glenn took this stance out of principle, assuming that his work would speak for itself, or was just weary of the effort in Florida. Nevertheless, it provided Collier an opportunity to remove an individual who was known to be at odds with his policies. Like many other critics of the Indian New Deal of the 1930s, Glenn believed that Indian total self-determination would hinder socioeconomic improvement of the tribes.

The letter presented here, ostensibly written to his niece Mary Jo in Tampa some eleven years following his apostolate, was apparently never sent. A unique and valuable historical document, it is the personal account of an Indian Service officer who was active in the field at the agency level during the tumultuous era around 1935, when national Indian policy was undergoing radical transformation. His candid, and not always objective, observations on the inadequacies of policies and programs formulated by the New Deal bureaucracy add another dimension to that preserved in the official records of the period. Furthermore, he provides valuable insights into the state of the Seminole culture during the Great Depression and the survival adaptations that the Indian people were forced to make. In another respect, Glenn's letter is also an important addition to the literature of Florida's social history, for the narrative indicates that a wide range of issues and numerous significant figures in the state had at least some impact on the Seminoles. Thus they were never as fully out of the mainstream of life as many writers have implied.

Some readers may view this letter as Glenn's belated attempt to vindicate his role in carrying out the federal policies of the 1930s. Indeed, his positions (such as the effort to acquire more land) sometimes proved to have been farsighted. Some readers may be offended by Glenn's occasionally ethnocentric language, but it is only reflective of national attitudes towards Indians half a century ago. Actually, Agent Glenn presents a complex amalgam of traditional assimilationist rhetoric and federal paternalism combined with an appreciation of Indians as individuals. In this respect he differed significantly from most other Christian ministers, who saw little in the Indian life-style worth retaining. Although Glenn felt that their once proud culture had been debased through poverty and forced contacts with a low stratum of white society, and that the Indians must adapt to modern ways to survive, he also hoped that the nobler elements of their traditional values might be retained. This was the same unrealizable dream of countless reformers who worked among the tribes, including Commissioner John Collier.

The letter has been reproduced essentially as James L. Glenn wrote it, with only minor editorial styling changes to facilitate reading. A few notes have been appended to identify significant historical persons and events for readers unfamiliar with Florida history. The letter is part of the James L. Glenn Collection of documents, manuscripts, and photographs donated to the Fort Lauderdale Historical Society by Dr. Glenn, who now resides in retirement at Rockwall, Texas.

Harry A. Kersey, Jr.

To Mr. and Mrs. Frank Stranahan
and
Mr. and Mrs. George W. Storter,

worthy members of that hardy race of men and women

who have made America possible

Dear Mary Jo:

I have your letter in which you ask me to give you a story of my work among the Seminoles of Florida. Perhaps I can best do this in the form of a letter to you.

One of our first delights as children is to go home with a neighbor boy or girl and see how he or she lives. If the home is different from our own, we are all the more interested in it. With a number of pictures I will take you to see some of the homes of our Indian neighbors which are very, very different from our own and which should prove interesting to us. Photograph number one shows one of these.

Since these people have no saw mills and therefore no lumber they do as our fathers did. They hew their houses out of the forest. The trees here are not oak or pine, but cabbage palms. This circle of huts has been called a village, but in reality it is a single house with eight or more rooms. The walls of the house are six posts, which support a palm leaf thatched roof, and a floor that is made of half-logs. This floor is about two-and-one-half feet above the ground. They do not "go into" their houses, but either sit about the sides of this floor or lay down upon it. But each hut has its own special use in "housing the family." Let us examine some of those shown in this picture.

The one at the extreme left is the pantry. Although the Seminoles are hunters they have always relied, in part, on garden and grain products for food.[1] In this hut the family keeps its seed for the next year's planting, its lard, dried meat, and other household supplies.

The second hut on the left is the sewing room. The women of this home are genuinely feminine in their love of pretty clothes. They design and make the most gorgeous of all human costumes. The dress or shirt is made of many, many color patterns, each of which is sewed to others in the same manner that our mothers worked out the color scheme of a quilt. In one of their skirts which I own are eight different colors of cloth, and twelve hundred different pieces. From twelve to eighteen yards of cloth are used in making it. Some of the patterns are not more than one-half inch square. I own a man's shirt that contains eighteen hundred seventy separate pieces of cloth, and eleven different colors.

These garments are made with a small hand-driven sewing machine. The seamstress sits cross-legged on the floor of this hut, with her machine and cloth in front of her, and turns the crank on the heel of the machine with one hand, and guides and feeds the cloth into the machine with the other hand.

So you see that this room in Billie Stewart's home is a very important part of his house, and that the women of this family spend many work hours in this room, making the clothing for the several husbands, daughters, and sons who live here.

The third hut from the left in this photograph is the dining room. Strangely enough the dining room floor and the dining room table are one and the same platform. The food in the pots and pans in which it was cooked is placed in the center of this platform and the members of the family sit on the outer edge of the platform with their feet hanging over the side to the ground while they eat.

We will have another picture of this table, together with its food, "china, silverware," and what not, but they always have a pot of soupy grits at hand, which they call sofkee, and from which all at the table use a

1. The Seminoles were traditionally subsistence farmers who cultivated small garden plots at their secluded camps. The fertile hammocks of the Everglades supported such crops as corn, beans, pumpkin, and bananas, which the Indians supplemented by hunting, fishing, and gathering wild edible plants. By the 1930s much of the game in the region had disappeared as a result of drainage projects and overhunting by whites, and the Indians increasingly purchased their staples from stores operated by white families.

1

common dipper to drink this semi-liquid.

The grits, itself, may be made from corn that is grown in a nearby garden, either by pounding it with mortar and pestle made of cypress, or a white man's hand-powered grist mill, or it may have been bought at the store of some white Indian trader. They also buy corn meal, flour, or loaf bread. They serve biscuits, sweet potatoes, honey, fish, pork, venison, wild turkey, pumpkin, comptee, which is made of a starch-packed root, gopher or land terrapin, turtle, heron or other water fowl, or "swamp cabbages," which is made of the bud of the young cabbage palm. They are fond of coffee and often sweeten a single cup with some four teaspoons full of sugar. For all of the above mentioned foods, they are poverty stricken, and often do not find enough to eat. When any people are really and truly hungry they do not stop to ask if the food meets government regulations for sanitation. The Seminoles may, and often do, eat semi-decayed meat, or other unwholesome food.

In the center of this circle of huts is a thatched roof supported by four posts. It has no floor in it, and is the kitchen. Here is the camp fire upon which is cooked the food, and about which the many cooks in the home gather.

One time when I visited Annie Tommie's kitchen I gathered up a lot of waste paper that she had scattered over the camp site and put it on her fire. She was one of our finest. With no protest at what I had done she carefully pulled the paper out of the fire and burned it a few pieces at a time. You see she knew that the flames from the fire that I was about to make would have reached up to the roof and burned the whole thing down. Fire prevention in a Seminole kitchen was something I had not thought about. They have a unique way of controlling the heat of their cooking stoves, which I shall describe later.

The men in the household often help in cooking the meal. They get the water, or put on the coffee, or fry the meat, or adjust the logs of the fire. Of course there is the same kindly interest between the husband and his wife, or wives, that we know in our homes.

Beside the several huts which I have already described in this picture there are four or five bedrooms. In general the family is divided during its sleeping hours as our own are divided. However, since they sleep with their clothing on they are less self-conscious about their bed fellows. We have spoken of both husbands and wives in a single household. Please don't think that one wife may have several husbands, even if, occasionally, one husband does have more than one wife. It is the law and custom of these people that the bride shall bring home her bridegroom to live in her father's household, or perhaps we ought to say her mother's household, for it is the mother's name that is not changed at marriage.[2] Billie Stewart and his wife were head of this family. If he had four girls and five

2. Glenn was not a trained ethnologist, and his descriptions of the Seminole family relationships here and the marriage ceremony (later in the letter) fail to point up some very important distinctions between the nuclear and the extended family. It is important to understand that in most Indian cultures the nuclear family marriage couple was not as important as the extended family matrilineal kinship group; thus both marriage and divorce were accomplished easily and without much fanfare. Moreover, children were not stigmatized by illegitimacy or by divorce of the par-

boys, his girls would each bring her husband to live with Billie Stewart. A new bedroom was built for the new bride and groom. His five boys would each go out of his home and live with his mother-in-law and father-in-law. As children were born to these sub-family groups they had to have bedrooms, and so other shacks were added to the circle that made up the whole of the house.

If Billie Stewart had had two wives, as a few Seminoles did have, and all the daughters of these two wives started these sub-family groups, each of which had children, I can imagine that home life became pretty ▼▼▼▼▼▼▼▼▼▼▼▼▼▼▼▼▼▼▼▼▼▼▼▼▼ ents, because they stayed within the matrilineal kinship group. Among the Seminoles this took the form of the "camp," comprising several generational households related matrilineally by clan. As noted, a newly united couple would set up a household in the camp of the wife's mother, and their children would be nurtured and instructed by the kinsmen of their mother. Their biological father, in turn, would be performing similar duties for the children of female members of his own clan.

badly mixed up. I knew a few cases where the "woman in the house" ordered the man out and made him go. I also knew of women who refused to be one of two wives, and who "walked out on the man" when he brought home a young and "beautiful bride" and asked that she become wife number two. I have also known of parents who were so dissatisfied with a new son-in-law that they descended on him, took his young bride away, and re-installed her in their household. And finally I have known of a young man marrying an old man's wife, and "getting away with it," and then marrying this wife's daughter, and keeping both of them. Lest we exult over such things, a thousand such irregularities in our marriage laws are found year in and year out even in our so-called "best families."

This strange Indian "house" would be incompletely described, however, if I failed to mention the platform at the base of the nearest palm tree which is shown in the photograph. It is a catch-all, much like our own poor kitchen tables. Pots and pans may be piled on it to bask in the sun light, or products from the garden or field may be thrown

here, or a saddle from a horse may rest here.

Back of these huts is the farm plot which this family cultivates. It contains eight or ten acres, and since it is hammock land it will grow corn, sugar cane, sweet potatoes, pumpkins, or other such products. No fertilizer is needed. It must be remembered that the Indians are not farmers, and that farming in Florida is a more specialized industry, I was about to say than making atomic bombs. At least the farmer's investment often "explodes" with considerable destruction. If the most highly skilled farmers of our own mature race fail at it, is it likely that these primitive people would make much of a success of it? On my first visit with the Indian Commissioner in 1931,[3] I urged upon him an in-

▼▼▼▼▼▼▼▼▼▼▼▼▼▼▼▼▼▼▼▼▼▼▼▼▼

3. Charles J. Rhoads, a Quaker humanitarian and banker from Philadelphia as well as president of the Indian Rights Association, was appointed U.S. Commissioner of Indian Affairs in 1929. During his administration there was a concerted effort to reform federal Indian policy along the lines recommended by the Meriam Report of 1928. It would seem that the Commissioner was favorably impressed with Glenn during their brief

dustrial program for these stranded tribesmen, but I had had too much experience with farming in Florida to believe that they could make a living by farming. I was most certain, however, that unless the Indian Service did discover some way for them to support themselves, their wives, and children the whole Florida Indian Service program was a farce. These small farms were extremely valuable because they were fertile, and the Indian knew how to use them as a supplement to his subsistence. One of my very distressing disappointments came to me when I found that, although Mr. Roy Nash, who made a social survey of the Seminoles in 1930,[4] was as deeply and as sincerely interested in them as I have been, and although he proposed certain half-hearted plans for their industrial re-establishment, in reality he believed their future was utterly hopeless. Notwithstanding, I still believed that something could be done for them, and that something must be done, and I urged this both in Washington and in Florida through five years of the most difficult work a man ever undertook.

We will have more to say about this later, but the little farm at Billie Stewart's home was the one I showed Dr. W. A. Hartmann, regional director of the Resettlement Administration,[5] when he and I began on a plan to set up a rehabilitation project for the Florida Seminoles. It was a beautiful spring morning, and the whole of this Indian Prairie country was most inviting. Billie Stewart had a fine field of corn, and an excellent garden. Dr. Hartmann not only failed to concur with Nash in the opinion that nothing could be done, but he said that here was an opportunity for the U.S. Indian Service to create the best of all its Indian communities. Hartmann was one of the young, progressive men who had both the vision and the courage for the work in which he was engaged, and he gave me his best in this joint undertaking.

This second picture, photograph two, was taken several miles north of the Ft. Pierce-Okeechobee road. Here a group of Indians

---

meeting in 1931, and expedited Glenn's appointment to the Florida post. Correspondence indicates that Rhoads was generally supportive of Glenn's work in the field. Rhoads was replaced as Commissioner in 1933. S. Lyman Tyler, *A History of Indian Policy* (Washington: Government Printing Office, 1973), pp. 116–22.

4. Roy Nash, an Indian Service appointee, was sent to survey conditions among the Florida Indians in 1930. His report to the Commissioner of Indian Affairs was published by the Senate the following year. During the period of his survey Nash used the title Special Commissioner to Negotiate with the Indians. U.S., Congress, Senate, *Survey of the Seminole Indians of Florida,* S. Doc. 314, 71st Cong., 3d sess., 1931.

5. In April 1935, President Roosevelt announced that by executive order several existing New Deal programs would be consolidated into a Resettlement Administration. This new agency, to be headed by former Undersecretary of Agriculture R. G. Tugwell, was to coordinate land classification, retirement of submarginal acreage and relocation of its residents, as well as a general rural rehabilitation program. In 1936 the agency became part of the Department of Agriculture and was renamed the Farm Security Administration. Paul E. Mertz, *New Deal Policy and Southern Rural Poverty* (Baton Rouge: Louisiana State University, 1978), pp. 124–26, 162–64.

2

had found the swamps impassable enough to keep away, largely, the white people, and enough hammocks, such as this one, to grow their necessary field products. It is my understanding that the Indians cleared this land, and farmed it; but when I took this picture a white family had built a hut here, and had planted this crop.

However, this field is almost exactly like that of Billie Stewart. He had cane, corn, sweet potatoes, pumpkins, and other products. In the past history of the Seminoles the farming was the task of the women of the household. It is natural that there should be a division of labor between the men and the women in any home. Since the men at times travelled as much as twenty miles per day on foot in search of game, it fell to the women, who stayed at the camp, to take care of the growing crop. Although they work very hard, they have a respected place in the family. Often when the "men folks" are drunk the women take over the task of keeping order, and at times tie up their drunken husbands or brothers with ropes.

When I first began my work with them I was told that the Indians at the reservation were in the habit of disturbing the Christmas entertainment because some vice-loving white men had made them believe that getting drunk was the way to celebrate this holy day. As soon as our Indian school began its Christmas program one of the young men showed up as drunk as they usually got. I told him that he could not go into the school house so long as he was intoxicated. He wanted to fight me about it, but his own people rushed to my defense, and took him away.

At another time another young man drank some rubbing alcohol and was almost insane when he rushed up to me and asked me if I was his friend. I had nursed the boy through a serious illness and had done a lot for him that I could not hire anyone else to do. I told him that I had been his friend. Because I was not afraid of him he rushed away from me and ran my white helper into the garage, but he then thought better of this idea of fighting either of us, and grabbed a large pipe wrench out of the shop and ran down another young Indian boy. He struck this boy across the back with the wrench, but he was immediately overpowered by both the men and women of his own people, and the women tied him hand and foot and watched over him until he was sober.

At the annual Green Corn Dance,[6] these same Indian women often have four or a half-dozen tied up with ropes until they are no longer violent. On the other hand the Indian wife is supposed to carry the burden for her husband. The dairymen at Dania used to give their day-old calves to the Agency Indians. The wife and not the husband carried

6. The Green Corn Dance, the primary religious observance of most Southeastern Indian tribes, is celebrated in the late spring by those observing traditional ways. Originally a series of ceremonies lasting several days, it was a time for fasting, spiritual renewal, ceremonial dancing, the naming of adolescents, and the administration of tribal justice. In Florida, the central figure in this ritual was the medicine man, supported by a council of elders for each band of Seminole and Mikasuki people. William C. Sturtevant, "The Medicine Bundles and Busks of the Florida Seminoles," *Florida Anthropologist* 7 (May 1954): 31–70.

the calf to the camp. But the men are not lazy. I had as many as fifty Indian men employed in some of my government projects. It was a common thing for the men who took their work seriously to say to me, "Bill—he no work today. He stand around too much. He get money he work" (he ought to work).

Paul, in one of his famous letters, said, "We wrestle not with flesh and blood but with principalities and powers." Motherhood in our own race is compelled to carry on when it seems that the task is beyond all human strength. The third picture of this series, photograph three, is to my mind a type picture of Seminole motherhood. In the background may be seen the wastelands of the Everglades, and you may guess how destructive to life it really is. Vast stretches of rock and water interspersed with all but impenetrable sloughs, almost devoid of any food-producing plants, but covered with saw grass, and growing an abundance of water moccasins; with no roads and few trails, and no sign posts, or even so much as land marks, with the grocery or drygoods store many, many miles away; a region which is largely non-tillable and at times is flooded

3

with water, wherein the game supply grows less and less with each passing year, where there is frost at times, and frequently an all but devastating hurricane. In such a region she sings her lullaby over her baby "Sleep my baby sleep" or carries him on her own strong back and shoulders as is doing this mother in this picture. She not only defends him from the blasts of storm, the ravage of disease, and the pain of famine but she is the only grammar school, high school and college he will ever have. Without books or news print she must glean from nature and from folklore whatever wisdom the "ages may have for her offspring." And strangely enough what was true and wise for her, in her childhood, is no longer wise and true today. Like the Old South her old world has gone with the wind, and she, herself, is a stranger in the new world about her. On several occasions, when I have been lost, I have found her in her own travel through the glades and she has guided me to my destination. Any one who comes to know her and her work comes to honor and respect her.

The fourth picture in this series shows some of her kitchen equipment. The block is from a cypress tree and has been hollowed out so it will hold about a quart of corn. The cypress pole is used to pound this corn into grits or meal. With this she must manufacture these items for her household.

In the fifth picture she is washing her clothes, or those of her family. This is a bridge across a canal. The water is crystal clear, and abundant. She probably has some soap, and after dipping the garment in the water, she beats the dirt out of it with this club that she has in her hand. The Indian families are like white families in that some of them are clean and careful about their children's clothing, and others are dirty and careless. They are a modest people, and strangely enough, the women are greatly embarrassed if they are seen in public without these beads about their necks. They wear no underclothing, and so have a costume that is both cool and conceals their persons. They usually go barefooted, and have a total of about five dollars invested in their dresses. But some of them may wear at least thirty dollars worth of beads and bracelets. In as much as her husband may invest sixty percent of his income in his rounds of drunkenness, she is surely entitled to whatever extravagance she may indulge in by the purchase of jewelry.

We still have other pictures later in this series that show us the kind of homes they have made for themselves in the Everglades. You might be interested in going to see the U.S. Indian Agency[7] and seeing what we offer them for this kind of living that you have already seen.

This sixth picture is a combination residence and administration building. It has two apartments in it, a guest room, and two offices. It is a lovely home, and for people who work as hard as these Indian Service em-

▼▼▼▼▼▼▼▼▼▼▼▼▼▼▼▼▼▼▼▼▼▼▼▼▼▼▼▼▼▼▼▼▼

7. The Dania Reservation, opened in the fall of 1926, was originally planned as a camp for sick and indigent Indians from throughout the South Florida region, but it quickly became a home for those Seminole families who had been displaced from their old camp sites along the lower east coast. The original agency built by Glenn's predecessor, L. A. Spencer, included a two-story combination office building and living quarters for government employees, ten two-

ployees it is not a luxury. These employees pay rent for their quarters as other people do.

However, it was a mistake to combine these several buildings into a single structure, for the reason that it had the appearance that the white employees were spending everything on themselves. The Indians, themselves, were quick to feel this, and the hundreds of tourists who visited the Agency would believe nothing else.

The Indians at the unit had such inadequate houses that my efforts were turned at once to giving them something better. Betty Mae was one of the bright and attractive young students in our school, and lived in a white squatters abandoned home. The house

▼▼▼▼▼▼▼▼▼▼▼▼▼▼▼▼▼▼▼▼▼▼▼▼▼▼▼▼▼▼▼▼▼

room cottages for the Indians, as well as a school, a wash house, and utility buildings. The reservation living area had an austere institutional aura which Glenn set out to alter through a renovation program. The community's name was changed to the Hollywood Reservation in the 1960s, and both the Seminole Agency and the Seminole Tribe headquarters are located there. Senate, *Survey of the Seminole Indians of Florida*, pp. 70–71.

4

5

6

was rotting, leaked in every room, and was infested with rats. I got some lumber together, wrecked the old house, and built her family a nice little cottage. She was naughty one day and I said, "Betty Mae, you must not treat us that way, we have built you a nice home." She answered, "You no build upstairs." In other words the white employee had the best home in which to live.

Picture number seven shows you what Betty Mae was talking about. You have heard the rhyme, "Ten little Indians, all in a line. One got drunk and then there were nine." Or did something else happen to this tenth Indian? Anyhow here are ten Indian houses all in a line, and if you had to live in Florida in a house ten feet by eighteen feet, and half of that porch, you would say most emphatically that they were little, and you surely must agree that they are in a line. I don't know who would be so miserable as to squat in one of these holes. You see that last house beyond the row, and do you recognize that big fire place chimney? That's the boss' house. No wonder Betty Mae was unimpressed with her new cottage.

Whatever else the Indian may lack he is never short on pride. He doesn't have to be told that he is as good as any white man. He knows that he is better. Their Genesis chapter one explains this clearly. "A long, long time ago the Great Spirit planted some seeds in a great river valley. By and by these seeds sent up hands through the soil, and God took hold of one, pulled on it, and out came a man. The Great Spirit told this man to go down to the river and wash the soil off himself. He went into the water, and washed and washed. When he came back he was pale and white. The Great Spirit called him the white man. But God was disappointed with this first try and grasped another hand from his field and pulled out another man. He told him to go and wash, but not to take all his vigor and strength away by over washing. But this second man was lazy a whole lot to begin with, so he did not wash any, but came back with the dirt still in his skin. He was the black man. But the Great Spirit tried again, and this time the man washed just right. He was red, strong and full of vigor. He was the Indian."

I do not know of anything in all of life of greater joy than to see a dream that one has cherished for a long, long time come true. You see the government is not allowed to build houses for the Indians, even though it did build a very many houses for its white citizens in recent years. How these dog huts were built in the first place without violating the laws that control government expenditures no one seems to know.

But one day I discovered that some race track barns were being sold in a nearby town. These barns had about fifty thousand feet of lumber in each, and they were selling for fifty dollars each. I had a building fund of eight hundred dollars allotted to my jurisdiction. I asked the Washington office for authority to use this eight hundred dollars for the purpose of rebuilding the Indian homes on the Agency grounds. When I signed the check for one of those barns I was so excited that I could barely write out the check, for I knew that if I got that barn my dream would come true.

We moved these cottages about a hollow square, and made each into a building eigh-

7

teen feet by twenty-four feet. The house shown in picture number eight is a little hospital that I built at a later date, but it is the same size building that each family had after almost a half of a year's work in rebuilding this set up.

And so as I sat in my living room one afternoon and watched my crew at work from the window I saw the last load of rock go into the drive way that led down, across, and back up from the complete Indian village. I thought, "It's been a long wait, but that's it." Perhaps it was because I had so much pride in my own race that I felt so humiliated with what we were offering those who came to us for a better life.

It is a long, long way from the equipment shown in pictures four and five to this tractor and plow, which are shown in my ninth picture. And if any man ever appreciated this fact it was Josie Jumper, who is refueling his tractor. He ran this machine for more than a year, and although it was a man-killing job he got as much work out of it as any white man anywhere.

The reservation that we had gotten for a home for our wards was matted with so much palmetto that the several hundred acres would barely support a dozen animals. A hurricane had killed a lot of the timber on it. We were authorized to use some funds in a program to clear it of this dead timber and palmetto. But the matter of getting this palmetto off Florida land is most difficult. The people who made the Reo automobile had invented some machinery that was supposed to do the work, but they spent more on their machinery than I had for my whole project. I began with a big plow and two Fordson tractors, one chained in front of the other. But the Indian who drove the front tractor would not keep his chain tight, and this just would never get anything done. I drove for seven days in search of some kind of a power plant to do my work. A capitalist had invested a fortune in a Florida farm, and had bought this five-ton Holt tractor. His farm did not pay, and he was ready to sell what he had for what he could get out of it. I offered him two hundred dollars for the tractor, and one hundred twenty-five for a seven-foot road grader. I took the blade off of the table of the grader, and bolted my heavy plow on it, and used the tractor to pull the grader. The new outfit used fifteen gallons of gas per day whereas the Fordsons had used twenty. I spent about one hundred and fifty dollars repair on the Holt, and a thousand dollars repair on two Fordsons in the time we used this machinery.

Both in the purchase of 50,000 feet of used lumber for fifty dollars, and in this buy of a tractor that cost, when new, between three and four thousand dollars, I felt that I had worked out the problem of the Florida Agency without too much help or interest from the Washington office. I was amused when I heard an official from Washington telling some of the people of Florida how "we" rebuilt the Indian villages at Dania, but when one of these same officers mocked my claim that this tractor cost, when new, anything like three thousand dollars, I was like the old Indian who, when his word was disputed, answered, "I say no more." One comes to endure a very great deal of impatience with the brass hats of the Indian Service, men who know everything.

Josie was never more delighted than when he tied this tractor to a large pine stump, and watched it drag the great roots out of the soil.

8

For about a year we had over a hundred Indians living on the reservation, and engaged in an industry that would last throughout the future. It was not only a training school in the use of machinery and in converting wastelands into useable wood lands and pastures, but it knit these people into a more compact community life, and gave them greater strength to meet the impact of white customs.

Josie's tractor had the power and the weight to do the work required of it, but Andrew Jackson had one of the Fordsons, and he soon discovered that his machine had neither, and that it also had the dangerous trick of turning itself upside down. If Indians have any claim to being good horsemen Andrew was the best rider of a pitching tractor that ever sat on a Fordson. He rode all over that machine and made it do its maximum work in spite of its wicked habits. He knew how to use the momentum of the weight of the machine to make it work for him, and he knew the exact split second when this momentum was used up and he had to release his clutch or be pinned under the thing.

Andrew was a perfect "Lone Ranger" type. He was tall and powerful, and a very likeable young man, even if he was tangled up in some of his habits. I put a lot of pressure on my workmen at the Agency to keep them from using their wages for whiskey. It is true, of course, that there were many white P.W.A. workers that got no more out of their government's help than another shot at liquor, and in spite of my best efforts there was some drinking in my crew. But Indians were good to report it to me, and I dispossessed the drunkard of his fire water. Andrew, himself, got happy one day, and when I found him he had two quart bottles, one in each hand, and a pint in each hip pocket. I told him I would send him to the county jail if he did not give me his liquor, but that did not impress him. He looked like Goliath to me, but I knew with the utmost conviction that Andrew would never strike me. I said, "Andrew, give me that whiskey." He stood before me with the two bottles raised as high as he could reach. But even though he was tall I was able to turn each bottle upside down while he held on to it, and pour the stuff on the ground. I slipped the two bottles out of his pockets and "spilled" them. He said nothing until I started back to my office, and then he rushed up behind me and said, "What fur you spill my whiskey?"

Charlie Buster was another excellent worker. He was dependable and always expected to do a day's work for his pay. One night he reported to me that two of the young boys had some whiskey and were drunk. But Charlie, himself, was drunk, and wanted to cover up by reporting on the boys who gave him his liquor. When I went after the two boys they ran back up into the woods and I lost them. Charlie came down on me and began mouthing around about letting the Indians "drink all the time." That was the last thing I wanted him to believe, and so I said, "Alright, Charlie, you are drunk yourself. You will go with me to the county jail." Charlie clenched his fist, and wanted to hit me as badly as any man I have ever met. But Charlie, not even when he was drunk, would violate the code of a Seminole. He relaxed and spent the night in jail. When I went after him I thought he would be mad at me, but he met me with a smile on his face, and said,

9

"Jail alright, good bed, good food." One loves men like that.

The only Seminole whom I encountered who would have broken their code was one who had come to the Agency and worked for a few days. On a Sunday he was drunk. He wanted to break into a cottage and disturb a sick Indian woman. The Indians had locked the door to keep him out. I did not know he was drunk until I saw him go to his own camp, get his axe, and with it raised over his head make for the locked door. I rushed out back of my house to get the sick woman's brother to help me handle him. We ran together to him, and since I did not mean to fight him I stopped near him and waited for the young Indian giant to block him. But the boy missed him, and he gave me one look, raised his axe and started toward me. I showed him neither anger nor fear, but stood my ground to await what would come next. The young Indian followed him up, gave him one blow on the side of his head, and staggered him. He dropped his axe and went back to his own camp. These were a few of the sensational features of our labor project. Unfortunately the constructive part of it is not so obviously dramatic. But one of the federal officers of the state set-up visited and inspected the work we had done. He said that our Indian workmen had accomplished more than was accomplished by white workmen on other projects; he only wished that he had as much to report on the most of the state projects as he found done there.

If I had waited long and dreamed much of rebuilding the Indian village at Dania, and the setting up of the kind of work program which I have just described, my deepest dream of them all was to find a dependable basis for a new Seminole industry. For extreme poverty is the most basic of all human ills, as many soldiers, returning from the prison camps of Germany and Japan, knew only too well.

The tenth picture shown here gives me some happiness because these Indian women have found work on a nearby farm and have fitted into the industry about them. They are picking peppers, and I am told that they were more careful in handling the vines than either white or Negro labor. Like so much farm work, they were employed only a few weeks of the year, but it does help them provide for their homes.

They are not fitted for so much of the work that their white neighbors do. The women would never be hired to cook, or care for a home, and none of them could do office work. The men are good mechanics, and some of them are working as auto mechanics. They are the best of guides, and hunters, but unless the Everglades National Park becomes popular, and there are tourists who will hire them as guides, the hunting schedule belongs to the past and not the future.

For many reasons I believed that we should work toward the establishment of two Indian communities in Florida. One of these should be located in the Indian Prairie country,[8] and

8. Indian Prairie is a broad expanse of grazing land extending to the west and north of Lake Okeechobee. These prairies are broken by islands of high pine and hardwood hammock vegetation, and extensive areas of pure cabbage palm. It is wetter than the Kissimmee River prairies to the north during the rainy season, but still represents some of the best grazing area in Florida. In the 1930s only a few cattlemen ran their herds on the

the other should be established in the best grazing area of the west border of the muck and south of Clewiston. Between Clewiston and the Hendry County Reservation[9] is some excellent pasture lands. The Agency should be located between these two communities at, or a few miles west of, Clewiston. This region from Brighton to the land south of the Hendry county reservation is the Florida Indian country.

Picture number eleven is a typical scene on the 35,000-acre tract which I set up for purchase for the site of this northern community. I have heard Mr. Ernest F. Coe,[10] the sponsor of the Everglades National Park, rise to the seventh heaven in describing the beauty of this park country. But there is no park in all the nation that has finer and more exciting natural beauty than this region. A nationally known artist, on visiting it, was so overcome by its loveliness that she wept over it. But this region is not only beautiful, it is the best of farm plots for growing the kind of food the Indians have always produced. It is exceedingly well fitted by nature for this Indian population.

To understand the Indian Service situation in Florida one must know that, following the Seminole War, these tribesmen scattered their homes over the Everglades much like a covey of quail that has been flushed, and for the same purpose. Like quail they were being run down by the members of an expeditionary force of the United States Army. Each family tried to hide in the swamp so deep and so impassable that these soldiers could not find it, and so far removed from any other Indian family that if they discovered one family there would be no clue

eastern portion of these prairies, and most of the land was considered submarginal due to the drainage problems. Senate, *Survey of the Seminole Indians of Florida,* p. 15; Barbara B. Darsey, "Brighton Seminole Indian Reservation," typescript (WPA Writers Project of Florida, 1938), Florida Collection, University of South Florida Library, Tampa.

9. The Hendry County Reservation of some 17,000 acres, lying partly on the eastern border of the Everglades, formed the nucleus of what is today the Big Cypress Seminole Indian Reservation. The original land holdings for this reservation were purchased in the 1890s and were expanded by a presidential Executive Order of 1911. Senate, *Survey of the Seminole Indians of Florida,* pp. 66–70.

10. Ernest F. Coe came to Florida in 1925, settling in Coral Gables, and was soon associated with groups interested in preserving the natural wilderness of the Everglades region. In 1928 he organized the Tropical Everglades National Park Association, which spearheaded the drive for establishment of a national park. The Florida Legislature supported the idea, but it took two years for the bill to clear both houses of Congress. President Roosevelt signed the measure establishing the Everglades National Park in 1934, but there were no funds appropriated for land purchase due to the Great Depression. During the late 1930s and '40s, state and federal efforts succeeded in securing title to over a million acres, and the park was formally dedicated by President Truman on December 6, 1947. Ernest Coe, the acknowledged "father of the park," died on January 1, 1951. Charlton W. Tebeau, *Man in the Everglades* (Coral Gables: University of Miami Press, 1968), pp. 175–80.

10

11

which might lead to other Indian homes. At that time there had been no drainage of the Everglades, and Lake Okeechobee extended south and south-east of its present location. Its shore line ran south from Clewiston. This western shore line of the lake was the final retreat along which many of these families established their homes.

Today there are about a hundred families in the state. It has been more than a hundred years since the wars, but they are still lingering about the old home sites, and many of them want the government to buy the small tracts of land on which their fathers and grandfathers have lived. From the standpoint of a program of education, health, law enforcement, and the development of their industry this situation is impossible. How can any teacher reach some three hundred children so long as they are scattered over five thousand square miles of swamps! Ask the returning soldiers of the South Pacific about jungle locomotion. How can any doctor go to such a population! How, indeed, can any Federal or state program be taken to them!

The one thing that incensed me in all of these affairs was this demand that in the use of these moneys, appropriated for Indian Service, the white man's interests were to have first consideration, after which this step-child citizen might come second. As will be shown later, white towns are interested in the location of the Agency because the pageantry of Seminole life and dress is a never ending source of curiosity to the tourist trade of the state. If I could have the voice of a god just for one statement I would use it to say that all of this pageantry, this difference between them and us, is secondary. Basically and fundamentally we and they are members of one and the same human family. Moreover, the Indian population is a just and rightful member of the American citizenship, and as such is no step-child. If we do not use school funds to build a post office or a fair ground, we must not use Indian Service funds to promote the tourist trade in Ft. Myers. Moreover the people of this town know that Nash had sufficient reasons to recommend that this city should be dropped from the list of medical service stations. I fought that set-up in Miami because this fifty-thousand dollar per year business was intolerable

from the standpoint of the Indian. But, knowing what I do about the Florida situation, I think I would rather locate the Agency at Musa Isle than in Ft. Myers. If for no other reason, why should the Indians be dragged half way across the state for service by their own government unit?

I will say more about this exploitation of the Indian, but just as there is no better place to rear the children of a home than some fertile and prosperous ranch or farm, so also these "simple children of the forest" had best center their community life in these stock-growing regions about which I have spoken. Here they can build the "better Indian way of life" which will be permanent and a credit to the good citizenship of the state of Florida.

The artistic life of races and peoples always has running through it like a thread of gold the story of the exotic beauty of their lakes and streams. Even though the stream shown in the twelfth picture is an artificial one it is as lovely as the famous Suwanee River of Florida. That the Seminole has a temperament which apprehends this thing that we have called beauty, is obvious from the pageantry of his life and dress. In fact

12

they are far less materialistic than our own people.

When I began work with them I found an Indian woman in the hospital, who in a drunken joy ride had broken, among other things, her hip, and had been in the hospital for three months. Since I had about four thousand dollars per year to use on my hospital and medical program, and she, alone, had used up about six hundred dollars of it, I asked her physician to dismiss the case as soon as it was safe to do so. About a week later her brother came to me and when I looked at him the tears were running down his face and he was sobbing. I said, "Wilson, what's the matter?" He answered, "My sister, he dead." Well, that was something to get excited about. Had the doctor let her go too soon? Had I been too eager to save money? I asked, "Where is she, Wilson?" With his whole body gripped with his suffering, he pointed a trembling hand upward and said, "He up there." I answered, "Yes, I know, but where is *she?*" Again he said, "He up there." An investigation revealed that Wilson was misinformed. That his sister was not even sick. But I had discovered also that

to a Seminole a person is the living element within the individual and not the physical element.

This kind of people ought to have a large endowment of beautiful features within their homeland. This Indian Prairie Canal runs through this Indian Prairie Reservation. The thirteenth picture in this group shows this same canal at a point near the Okeechobee Lake. To the left of the picture is one of the finest herds of range cattle that I had seen in the state, but the beauty of this region "stole the show" in this photograph. The garden of flowers to the right is floating on the face of the stream.

This following story helps to reveal the artistic and religious temperament of the Seminoles. One night at the Agency I awoke after what seemed to me like a short sleep, and heard my door bell ringing. I rushed down to see who was calling and found Josie Billie with a party of Collier County Indians waiting for me. He explained that they had come to visit the grave of a relative, and wanted me to go with them to the cemetery. They explained that they had to go when the morning star was at a certain point in the sky.

So I drove up with them in the truck. When we gathered about the grave Josie said that this boy had been dead three months, one of the tribe's great leaders had been dead a hundred years on that night, and they now had a leader who was very old. They had come to this grave to honor these three members of their tribe.

Josie asked me, "I say something and then you say something?" He then spoke to those who had come with him, in the kind of speech that our own people make in such a ceremony, and then he talked to the Great Spirit about the welfare of their dead and their living. After which I told them how we honored our dead, and how we, too, thought that the important part of a person is the living part and not the physical part, and how we trusted a Great Spirit to take care of us and our dead.

Pictures fourteen and fifteen show some of the white man's mistakes which are expensive to him and to the Indian. The latter reveals what a fire does to the muck land. The dust I am pouring from my hand is as pure ashes as ever taken from any fireplace.

13

14

15

The foreground of the picture is a great bed of it. At my side are the banks of unburned muck.

Any map of South Florida will show a half score of canals running south and east from Lake Okeechobee through the muck section of the Everglades. This muck is twenty feet deep in some places. If this land had been drained, a small section at a time, and put under cultivation immediately as it was drained, this region would have been worth the half of a state in its productive capacity.[11]

Picture fourteen is supposed to show a muck fire, but the printing paper now available will not reveal the smoke. There is a hint of smoke on the horizon at the left of

▼▼▼▼▼▼▼▼▼▼▼▼▼▼▼▼▼▼▼▼▼▼▼▼▼▼▼▼▼▼▼▼▼▼▼▼▼

11. The State of Florida began a full-scale drainage of the Everglades in 1907 during the administration of Gov. N.B. Broward. Canals were cut through the Everglades from Lake Okeechobee to the lower east coast. These significantly lowered the water table of the region and took a terrible toll of animal and bird life that depended on the aqueous habitat. The ecological balance was upset, and the Everglades became more susceptible to long periods of drought.

this print. These fires break out in the dry season of the year and rage for weeks, or until some rain puts them out. They usually burn down to the wet muck, however deep that may be. Anyone who has fought a muck fire knows how difficult it is to stop one.

Although the Seminoles never cultivated muck land they hunted duck, and other water fowl on this lower part of Lake Okeechobee before it was drained away, and they fished from it. It also "fenced out" the white man from their hidden homeland. On the other hand they pole their canoes along these canals and trap raccoon and otter by their shore, and kill alligator and catch fish from them. On the whole, this drainage project of South Florida has been badly managed.

Talk, talk, talk, that was about all we ever did about setting up a new and sound industry for the Florida Seminoles. And this had to be done first or else all the other programs were a farce. One soon learned that the brass hats won't "stick their necks out" on tries that may fail. The one in the field must take the chance, and get the black ball if it doesn't work.

In about 1934 I got those few Agency Indians at Dania to go along with me in a crop of beans. We got about a hundred dollars out of them, and I got them to buy about a dozen of the wild range cows of Florida. We had already fenced the three hundred and twenty acres at Dania, and these cows did well on what pasture we had. But they did a lot more than that. They reassured our timid officials of Washington, and picture number sixteen shows what can be done when those men want to help. This is part of a herd of seventy-five or eighty purebred cows. In my opinion the purchase of this herd was the first sound and genuinely constructive thing the Washington office ever did for the Florida Seminoles.

16

After we had bought a part of the 35,000 acres in the Indian Prairie region on the north-west shore of Lake Okeechobee, I got about 1,200 head of Texas cattle from one of the relief agencies of the government.[12] The two herds were put on that range and I am told that in 1945 their surplus sold for $30,000.

These Agency Indians at Dania were promised a home there, and they have been the nucleus through which the government has developed its Florida program. They have been cooperative and faithful. They must not be let down. There was a track of muck near this reservation that I wanted but never got. It ought to be added to this property.

Photograph number seventeen means just a whole lot to me, not because these girls have gotten hold of some evening gowns from some white women, but because of these two sets of beautiful teeth, and two happy and healthful faces. They are Mary Tommie and Agnes Parker, two of our school children. I have often told the men of this tribe that there were many things that the white men had that they did not want their people to have, but education was one thing that they needed most of all. Because we are disgusted with ourselves and with the wars that curse the higher educated communities of the world, we have elevated men to high positions who are so misdirected in their convictions that, as John Collier[13] said to me, they are afraid to teach these Indians to read, for they then will read the newspapers and get in the awful world in which we live. In spite of his ecstasy over the glory and

---

12. In November 1935, two thousand head of cattle were made available to the Seminoles by Dr. Philip Weltner, regional director of the Resettlement Administration. According to Agent Glenn's annual report for that year, "Five hundred forty-seven were shipped immediately, and arrangements were completed for the shipment of another five hundred head. In the meantime, the Indian Office had rejected the final land program, and many of the cattle already received were starving to death because the lower grazing lands had not been purchased. The second shipment was abandoned." Thus it is difficult to account for the figure of twelve hundred head of cattle that Glenn cites in the letter. Also, in her study of the origin of the Seminole cattle industry, Merwyn S. Garbarino uses the figure of five hundred head of government cattle as the origin of the tribal herd. U.S., Bureau of Indian Affairs, *Annual Report, Narrative Section, 1935, Seminole Agency, Dania, Florida*, p. 14; Garbarino, *Big Cypress, A Changing Seminole Community* (New York: Holt, Rinehart & Winston, 1972), p. 126.

13. John Collier, a philosophical progressive, trained social worker, and executive secretary of the American Indian Defense Association, was the leading exponent of Indian self-determination during the 1920s and '30s. President Roosevelt appointed him to the post of Commissioner of Indian Affairs in 1933 with the expectation that Collier would bring about an "Indian New Deal." Collier more than met this expectation through his advocacy and implementation of the Indian Reorganization Act of 1934, which revolutionized federal relations with the tribes. His policies set a new direction for the American Indian people in

goodness of the primitive life, I think I have seen enough of it to be assured that it too has its "sweat, blood and tears."

In picture number eighteen we have some of these so-called "primitive children of the forest" unspoiled by the kind of training that other children have had. These kiddies were camped near Turner's River in Collier county. The one next to the end on the left is Horace Jumper, the first Indian I ever tried to interest in written languages. Josie Billie worked out an understanding with the several families concerned whereby I could run out from the

Town of Everglades, where I was then employed, and set up this class.

George W. Storter,[14] a very fine citizen indeed, says that one Indian brought him his boy and said, "I leave him here maybe one week, maybe two weeks. You teach him to read and write." Josie Jumper, who drove the big tractor for me, said, "My boy Moses, you take him, and fix him all the same as white man" (educate him).

The next picture, number nineteen, is one that I have kept in my own files. Let me

hasten to say that I have seen about as many flies on the table of white people as you see here. But to white people or Indians, it means death.

To adapt at my school to the immediate, primary, and basic needs of children like Mary Tommie and Agnes Parker I required the teacher to set up a class in cooking. The Indian Service provides the noon lunches for all Indian school children. I therefore asked them to cook that food, and in cooking it to learn not only cooking but sanitation. Collier's appointee who succeeded me took this

allowing them a greater voice in determining the rate and extent of acculturation they wished to undertake. By the time Collier left government service in 1945 he had become one of the most controversial figures on the national scene. Apparently Collier's view that Indians would not necessarily be benefitted by adopting some aspects of non-Indian culture, such as formal education, disturbed Agent Glenn. Glenn was firmly convinced that Seminole survival in the twentieth century was contingent upon at least a modicum of assimilation into the mainstream of the dominant society via education and job training, and

he vigorously encouraged young Indians in this direction. The resulting philosophical conflict between Glenn and Collier became more pronounced between 1933 and 1935, and ultimately was a cause of Glenn's dismissal from his position. For the definitive treatment of Collier's administration, see Kenneth R. Philp, *John Collier's Crusade for Indian Reform, 1920–1954* (Tucson: University of Arizona Press, 1977).

14. George W. Storter, a native of Alabama, moved to a site on Allen's River in 1887 and began a farming and lumbering enterprise. Within a short time he had opened a store to serve

other settlers and a trading post for the Mikasuki-speaking Indians who had their camps in the lower Big Cypress Swamp region. Storter became very successful in these ventures and was a prominent citizen on the southwest frontier of Florida. In 1922 he sold most of his holdings to Barron G. Collier (see note 17), and the town of Everglades which had grown up around the Storter homestead became the county seat of the new Collier County, formed in 1923. Charlton W. Tebeau, *Florida's Last Frontier* (Coral Gables: University of Miami Press, 1966), pp. 113–25.

17

18

food the government had bought for the lunch of these children and threw it in pots like these and turned them back to this kind of table sanitation. He disbanded the school, and entered them in the school at Cherokee, North Carolina.[15] The Florida school was an expensive affair, and in some ways these children learned faster after they were separated from their people. But it made more difficult the gap between these educated Seminoles and their own people, and there were a

smaller number of children who would go to school under these conditions.

The death rate among the children of the Seminoles was very high. When one goes, as I have done, back into the cypress or pine woods of some isolated region, and an Indian mother places in his arms her own sick baby, and he takes it and her to the hospital, and he and she leave it there, he wants it to get well very, very much. The bitterest thing he will ever have to do is to hunt up that

mother and say, "Your baby died." It is useless to say, "He would have died anyhow." She will always wonder if the Indian doctor might not have saved it.

Number twenty is a picture of the primitive man's "locker plant." This young girl has killed a hog and is drying some of the meat. A ham is suspended on the pole at the right of the picture. You will notice the split log platform that is the floor of their homes. These are palm logs, here, but in many cases cypress or pine is used.

I have lived in several white "company" towns, including a phosphate mining town of Florida. I have seen a lot of jealousy among white neighbors under such conditions. The U.S. Indian Service projects into the Indian community a like condition. On one occasion I had a milk cow which belonged to me personally. I told the Indians at the Agency they could have her if they would kill her and divide her among all the families at the Agency.

The Indian women killed her and gathered about her to dress her meat, but I discovered that Jim Gopher was not represented in the

15. The Seminole children who were sent to the Cherokee School in 1937 were confronted with massive culture shock. Not only were they separated from family and friends for the first time, and placed in an unfamiliar setting of a boarding school with Indian children from other tribes, but they also had to make adjustments to the forbidding climate of the North Carolina mountains. Despite these difficulties, two of the girls continued there for eight years and graduated from high school in 1945. These two graduates were Betty Mae Tiger and Agnes Parker, both of whom Glenn knew and mentions in his letter. Many other Seminole youngsters would attend the Cherokee School for varying lengths of time, and a few more graduated, until the boarding school was closed in the 1950s. Throughout this period the Seminole youngsters received a great amount of support from various civic groups, especially the Friends of the Seminoles organization in Fort Lauderdale headed by Mrs. Stranahan. *See* Harry A. Kersey, Jr., and Rochelle Kushin, "Ivy Stranahan and the 'Friends of the Seminoles' 1899–1971," *Broward Legacy* 1 (October 1976): 7–11; and Harry A. Kersey, Jr., "Federal Schools and Acculturation among the Florida Seminoles, 1927–1954," *Florida Historical Quarterly* 59 (October 1980): 165–81.

19

group. I went out to them and asked them if they had told Jimmy to send Ada or Mary down, and they said they had not. I found Jimmy all puffed up with anger. I said, "You go down there and share with the other families." His home was on a hill overlooking the group of women. As we looked down upon them they were all about the old cow, cutting the hide away as fast as they could. Jimmy said, "A bunch of buzzards." Jimmy overstated it just a whole lot, but I knew all too well how greedy they were for meat, and how this jerked meat, at times, spoiled on them, as it would on white people who had the primitive model of "locker plant." It is not something to laugh about but a thing of suffering and death

I told you early in this story that I would take you into their kitchen and let you see their cook stove. Number twenty-one is such a picture. This young girl is preparing her meal. The four logs project into a single point, and here the fire is kindled. The heat control of this cooking "range" is manipulated by pulling the logs in or out as the fire is to be made hotter or cooler.

They have no ovens, or pressure cookers. She must either fry or boil her foods. A few of them have an open fire oven in which they bake bread. They have no notion of the cause of disease, and therefore they are not greatly concerned with all this bother of sanitation. They are always burdened with white men prowling about their homes, but if you come to one of them as their guest, and you are too bigoted to eat their food, they are hurt, of course.

I arrived at the home of one of the least sanitary of them all about dinner time. The young women had been out hunting the swamps and ponds for food. One came in with a prairie terrapin, and without so much as killing it, pushed it head down in the camp fire. It shot out its legs as the flames killed it, and they stood around it and waited for it to roast. In the meantime I sat down at their table and thought I would eat some bread and honey. I said, "Oh, I want some of that honey." It was in a white hand basin, but I was reared in the cowboy country and was not disturbed over that. But when one of the women handed it to me, and I gazed through some very fine honey, I saw the dirt, grime, and grease that was caked on this pan when it had been used in washing their hands. I had seen pans get that way, and I had also seen a most diligent mother clean them up. I knew that they ought not to go with food.

Pictures twenty-two and twenty-three afford a contrast in what we commonly call progress, or a better life. The first of these is locomotion not in a jungle but in a prairie section of the Everglades. I have walked miles and carried groceries in a sack to sick Indians rather than fight this sand with an automobile. And yet I drove this car seventy thousand miles in eighteen months; I have cut logs and poles and carried them a mile to get my car out of a sand hole like this, or out of some swamp.

During the year, the Cow Creek Indians asked me to come to their Green Corn Dance for the purpose of discussing the land they wanted for a home. Willie King,[16] a Creek Indian from Oklahoma, and one of the most faithful and helpful men I had in all the Ser-

16. The Reverend Willie King, a Creek Indian from Oklahoma, was sent as a missionary to the Florida Seminoles in the 1920s. He was sponsored initially by the Creek, Seminole and Wachita Association of Indian Baptist churches in Oklahoma. To supplement this stipend he apparently was employed in some part-time capacity at

vice, and I drove from near Miami to the town of Okeechobee, and found that we had about twenty miles of swamp to make before we reached the camping ground. We managed to get through all the mud holes and shallow lakes until we got in about a mile of the place. And then there was no road. The whole region was covered with palmetto logs, and a number of fallen pines which were hidden by the leaves of the palmetto. There was two or three inches of water on the ground, and there was also a heavy coat of slime over it. We bumped over and skidded around logs, our back wheels spun and dug out the sand until the axle rested on the ground, a pine stump or palmetto log. We dug out, and tried again and again. After our engine was almost burned up with heat we came to a small stream which we either had to cross or get stuck in. Here we came upon

some fools who were fighting this road "just to see the Indians." At least that was the purpose of a young man and his wife. The driver of the car was drunk, and the young girl was both ashamed and frightened. Their car was already stuck in this stream, and we had to help them get it out before we could get by them. When the girl saw that I was a government official she ran up to me and said, "I want you to know that neither I nor my husband drink. We want you to know that we are not that kind of people."

The five of us pushed his car out of the hole, and then we all got my car across. We bumped across and skidded about another half mile of palmettos, unable to know at what time we would destroy a tire, knock off a wheel, or tear a hole in the oil pan of our engine. A short time after sundown we came

upon the camp. We could see it, but that final half mile was one of the most impossible roads I ever put a car over. It was a swamp with about six inches of water over a slime-covered bottom. The wheels had almost no traction on it whatever. The five of us left one car and pushed the other across. The girl did the driving and we did the pushing. When we got across our tongues were out, we were dripping with sweat, and our clothes were soaked with mud and water.

For all of our exhaustion we were in time for what must have been a great pageantry in the past. The warriors were returning to their campfires. But the ragged bunch of men whom I saw returning that night made one choke his tears back. There was no order, the yells were few and far between, and there were only a dozen or so left of a band which at one time must have been numbered by the thousands. Sam Jones, their leader whom we were to talk with, was drunk already. King and I had no official body to talk to. The council of the group had long since gone on the rocks. I had already spent a half-day trying to convince Sam Jones that he and his people ought to take whatever the government could be persuaded to give.

the Agency. In 1934 the Florida Baptist Convention began supplementing the salary of the Reverend Mr. King, and four years later the Home Mission Board of the Southern Baptist Convention also contributed to his support. King retired from his missionary work in 1945. Edward Earl Joiner, *A History of Florida Baptists* (Jacksonville, Fla.: Convention Press, 1972), pp. 154–55; Seminole First Baptist Church (Dania, Florida), *Dedicatory Service, May 29, 1949,* souvenir brochure, private collection of H. A. Kersey, Jr., Boca Raton, Fla.

20

21

22

23

The Indians were mad because this drunken white man had barged in on them without an invitation. I soon made up my mind that if I got myself and King out of there I would do well without trying to force him out of there, too. The girl and her husband said they would go with us, and so we hit the swamp again. By this time the girl's shoes were so wet that she pulled them off and her clothes were dripping with water. Driving a car in a swamp is not only difficult but it takes considerable knowledge of just how to handle it to get the most out of it. She was worth her weight in gold in the kind of character that counts most. She swung onto that wheel while the engine boiled and sputtered and the rear wheels shot up a fountain of mud and water. King was an older and a larger man than I but never in all the time I worked with him did he ever complain or do less than his part in these emergencies.

When we reached the palmetto again it was pitch dark and our headlights gave us even less knowledge of what was before us. I asked the girl to get in the cab because she was wet and I knew she would be cold, but she and her husband got in the truck behind the cab. We had gone about half of our way through this palmetto when I hit the hard and sharp end of a dead pine log and tore a great hole in the tire of the front wheel. We were so exhausted that if we had not been grown men I guess we would have all broken down and cried over our misfortune. The girl did break under the strain and began sobbing. I had been through too many such experiences to let myself go. I said, "We have two spares; take it easy; we'll get out of here." We pulled ourselves together, changed tires in the dark, and bucked this wasteland again. We reached Okeechobee at two o'clock the next morning and delivered the husband and that brave kid of his to their home. I have never seen them again but I bet they never forgot this trip or wanted to see another Green Corn Dance.

Number twenty-three is not the "white man's way." That is said so much that both the Indian and the white race get the notion that all progress is the exclusive possession of the white man, and all primitive and reactionary things belong to the Indian way of life. Great roads were built, perhaps, before there were any white men. This road was built in part by Indian labor, but largely by white labor, and wholly by the brains and tools of the white race. It is a section of the Tamiami Trail that was built from Tampa south to Naples and across the Everglades to Miami. It was not only a great engineering undertaking, but it required the kind of jungle work that was done by the army in the South Pacific.

The important thing about these two contrasting ways of travel is found in the fact that any race, white, red, brown, or black, has certain basic problems of progress which it must either meet or go the way of the dinosaur. The Indian has a way of life that will mean more to him than anybody else's way, but it, too, has degrees which lead from the lower to the higher forms of living. He must meet the problem of progress.

In pictures number twenty-four and twenty-five let us turn back again to the subject of beauty. The first of these is a picture of the town of Everglades, the county seat of Col-

24

lier County. This was the headquarters for the construction of the most difficult portion of the Tamiami Trail.[17] It is one of the most beautiful towns in the state. About sixty years ago George W. Storter and his wife made their home here on this river. After several tries at farming and what not they put in a general store and in the course of time the Seminoles came to trade with them. If all of the white men whom the Indians have known were as honest and as gentle as were these people, the dream of William Penn might have been realized.

When I lived there the Collier Company was under the management of D. Graham Copeland, who in his relation to the Indians was both fair and generous. He has not only given them employment, but he has also given them shelter, food, and medication.

The second picture shown [25] belongs to Mr. Ernest F. Coe's Everglades National Park dream. These, of course, are [African pink] flamingoes. There is only one flock in the state and they are far south of the Tamiami Trail. They are only one of the many types of water fowl that live both in the Indian country and the Park region. The wild turkey are being killed out. The Indians did make better money than any group of white people off the egret, but a law stopped that, and then they made up to twenty dollars per day from alligator pelts, and now they are almost gone.

17. Barron G. Collier (1873–1939) was one of those business success stories typical of the Gilded Age. A native of Memphis, Tennessee, he went to New York as a young man and by the turn of the century had amassed a fortune based on control of nationwide franchises for streetcar advertising. In 1911 he came to Florida for the first time, became infatuated with its beauty, and purchased an island property near Fort Myers. Each winter the family resided in Florida, and Collier became a legal resident of the state in 1926. Prior to that he had seen the potential for development and had begun acquiring tracts of land, until he controlled approximately one million acres in Southwest Florida. In 1923, the Florida legislature, after much intensive lobbying, passed a bill creating the new Collier County. The main inducement for securing the legislation was Collier's pledge to complete the cross-state highway known as the Tamiami Trail. This roadway running from Tampa to Miami had to cross the heart of the Everglades, thus presenting a major engineering and construction challenge. The man whom Collier selected to head this expensive project was David Graham Copeland, an engineering graduate of Rensselaer Polytechnic Institute and a naval officer during World War I. Construction of the Tamiami Trail through the county took five years. After the road was completed in 1928, Copeland resigned as chief engineer but remained as manager of the Collier properties until his retirement in 1947. Tebeau, *Florida's Last Frontier,* pp. 83–95, 207–208.

25

If you will go back to the first picture you will remember that, when we called on Billie Stewart, he and his family were not at home. Picture number twenty-six shows where they were. Some of the men of the household had gotten work in Brighton, and they had set up a "temporary camp" near that city. You will notice the temporary nature of the house. Two scrub oaks furnish a little shade, but this is an uncomfortable life.

This camping near a white labor market is a recent thing, but these people have always pulled about from place to place through the whole year. At one time they move to some huckleberry patch and pick these berries, both to eat and to sell. At another they move near a flock of wild turkey, or a herd of deer, or on some canal where otter or raccoon can be trapped. They tie their bed clothes in bundles, stuff their pots and pans in sacks, and pile their pigs, ducks or chickens, and dogs in the back seat of the old model-T and "high away" for some new, strange, and far away residence.

In cases of emergency I had to furnish transportation for these families, and these trips often turned out to be out of the ordinary. During a Florida hurricane I usually spent the day or night in trying to get to any family that might be in distress. The Indians knew just where I might be needed and would help me at such times. On one such trip I reached a stranded family after the "big blow" had ended. They were camped in a palm forest and the trees had crashed about them. They had taken refuge under the platform of a hut. The rain was almost heavy enough to drown them, the logs lay across the top of their shelter, and the water had covered the country for miles to a depth of from one to three feet. They were wet and cold. All of their food was gone. It was foolish to leave them in this wet hole, and since they were a hundred twenty-five miles from my home, there was little I could do for them there. I had a model-A Ford. I gathered up ten men, women, and children, besides these bundles of pots, pans, and bedding. Their animals were either drowned or had run away. In spite of wet roads, an overload, and other little things like that, we reached the Agency, where they had the care they needed.

On another occasion one of Miami's leading doctors said an Agency Indian had a tumor and must undergo an operation. Old Doctor McSwain of Arcadia was one of the greatest physicians of the state. I told the family that I would want to know what he had to say about it before I consented to the operation. The girl wanted her people to go with her to Arcadia, so we struck out for the Big Cypress country after her people. We found them near a canal, and they loaded themselves and theirs in my car. I had all the fenders loaded down with household supplies, and in the back seat I had four women, two dogs, and two ducks. There were four of us in the front seat. The springs of the old car banged together all the way to Arcadia and when we got there I spent another hour in finding a place where they might spend the night. In the meantime, Dr. McSwain examined the woman and reported that she would be a mother a few months later. To add to the work which I did for them, her husband was drunk the next morning, and I resolved that whoever that bootlegger was he would pay for it. And he did.

The doctor in Miami was a specialist and

26

not our regular doctor. He depended on an X-ray and the woman would not remain still for his picture. His mistake was that and no more. On the other hand, the Indians may not have appreciated the service I gave them, but this checking on possible mistakes is something I would want for my family and I tried to put myself in their place when such matters were to be decided. I had saved the life of the child and the cost of an expensive operation.

But this "highing away" for another and another place to live, this gypsy life they lead, adds thousands of miles to the driving that the Indian Service employees have to do. If we are going to give them a program, must we first run them all over one of the largest and most inaccessible swamps in the United States to get it to them? Sometimes these Indians go for three or four days, at least some of them, without having one bite to eat in their homes. It is not laziness. At times the woods are without any game, and there is no work for them.

One of their interesting stories runs like this: Many moons ago a great drought came to the home of the Peninsular People (the Florida Indians) and the deer and the turkey went far away. The streams dried up and all the fish died. The fire swept through the homes of the Indians and the pickaninnies and squaws get hungry *ojus* (very much).

An old Indian sees the Great Spirit in his dream and he is told that the Prince of the Happy Hunting ground will come; that he will land at the south tip of the country and will come through all the Indian homeland.

The old Indian goes many days to meet him and he finds him and they go all through the Indian home and sow comptee seed. And he shows them how to make comptee flour out of the roots of the comptee plant. After that the Indian always has something to eat.

But the story did not anticipate the day when the white man would dig up the comptee and make starch out of it.

If they might have two prosperous communities, where they would not have to expose their children to hunger, moisture, and cold, they would be better off and the U.S. program would be effective.

Photograph number twenty-seven is one of my favorites of them all. When I left the camp shown in number twenty-six, I came by these two kiddies. This is an "automobile" they are in. It has a dashboard, steering shaft, gear shift, and seat. That is enough to enable the imagination of these youngsters to supply the rest. I have worked with children all my adult life but I have never seen less play among any group than I found in the back country homes of the Everglades. Our school children, on the other hand, were as full of fun as any children I have ever known.

A movie version of one of the famous children's stories was given in Miami, and my wife took five or six of the Indian school children over to see it. The form of greeting as per the Indian way does not include the kiss. But in some part of this picture the two leading characters kissed each other. That aroused the humor of these girls. They would say, "He kiss her. Dirty *ojus*." And then one of them wrapped her arm around a young boy in the car and planted a loud kiss on his face. All shouted with laughter at this "funny" thing that the white people did.

The first time I saw this baby, the one in picture number twenty-seven, it was about

27

three months old. His mother had died sometime before, and the family was trying to feed him on solid food. His ribs protruded, his face had left his cheek and face bones jutting out, and his legs and arms were like the stem of the water lily. I talked the matter over with the family, and decided that it was no good to try to feed the child on bottled milk. I hoped that I could find a wet nurse for him. After hunting around for several days I found an Indian mother who had lost her baby a few days back, and I told Billie Stewart that I would pay the young woman to come to his place and nurse his grandson. He discussed the proposal with the women of his camp and came to me with the answer that "Indians don't do that way." I then bought a bottle and milk and told them to keep both these items clean and warm when feeding the child.

They did not do so bad at that, but he contracted an ear infection and I had to hospitalize him for several weeks. We only hoped that we could save him, but here he is. That he is part deaf is obvious from the look on his face.

One of the most difficult pieces of work that I ever did in my law enforcement program was in behalf of Charlie Snow, one of the young men who belonged to this camp. Charlie spoke good English, and these Indians depended on him a great deal. My first assignment was the prosecution of two drunken white men who ran into his model-T and wrecked it. The attorney at Okeechobee informed me that if I wanted pay for the Indian's car I would have to put up a civil suit, and if I got damages he thought the white men had no money. The civil suit would cost more than the old car was worth. But we did prosecute the men for drunken driving and they were fined and thrown in jail.

Charlie Snow thought that the state was a crook in that deal. It and not he got the pay for the wrecked car. A friend bought him a new model-T so it came out all right after all.

Billie Stewart and his family came to the Agency for work some time later, and as I looked over my evening paper I saw a story that reported that Charlie Snow was killed by a hit-and-run driver on the night before. I took the paper to them and they and I left for their home. Two Negroes had taken a white man's truck and gone to Okeechobee and as they returned, the fog was so heavy that they could not see the road. The driver was going at about fifty or sixty miles per hour. Charlie had parked beside the road and, after cranking his car, was coming around the side to get back in it. The front fender of the Negro's car hit him and killed him. The Negro was so badly scared that he speeded up his car instead of stopping.

There were plenty of Indian witnesses to tell the court what they saw, but I had no absolute proof that the driver was the Negro we had arrested. Only that other Negro could give us that information, and it was up to me to find him. I learned, after several days driving, that he had been employed by the Department of Agriculture in a project at the very south point of the state. I headed my car down into those wilds, but a deputy sheriff promised me that he would see that the Negro would not get out of there without me knowing about it. But I then discovered that he had already come out of there and had been in the hospital in Miami and was somewhere in Negro town of that city. I bursted into one Negro home after another until I found him. He went with me without any trouble, and after many months we convicted the driver and the Judge gave him two years in the penitentiary. It did not bring back Charlie, but the Stewarts were grateful for this measure of justice.

Picture number twenty-eight is old Johnny Buster. Billy Stewart had asked me to take him over on my relief program. He said the old man was eighty or ninety years old and his family had left him alone. I drove over to see him and he was both friendly and courteous. I said, "Maybe so you need some meat and flour." With a smile he answered, "Some Indians take them. I no take them." Translated it might run like this: "That's very kind of you and I appreciate it, but I would rather make my own living." There was not a cup full of food on his table, and he had on only this thin knee-length shirt. I said, "Maybe so you cold. Heavy coat I give you." He smiled again but said, "I no take them."

I said, "Alright, Johnny, you're a great guy. I wish I could say that if I ever get as old and ragged and hungry as you are. But I do want this wooden spoon you have, and I will give you two dollars for it." The Indian never sees those hidden purposes of the white man.

28

He took the two dollars and I took the spoon, knowing well enough he could make himself another.

Several days later I returned to Billie Stewart's camp and wanted him to go with me to talk to Johnny about this business of the necessity of a relief agency for men like him. One of the fanatics of Florida, who works both sides of the street and raises all the hell he can, lives at Ft. Myers. He had been in the camp, and had told Billie Stewart that I was letting all the Indians die. Billie was mad at me. He told me what had happened. I knew the Seminole story through a hundred years of history a lot better than Billie Stewart knew it. I said, "Billie Stewart, you people never know who your friends are. You believe this man today and that man tomorrow. You have never had anybody that has helped you more than I have, and that is over and above what I am just supposed to do." His face softened and he smiled and said, "I go."

There was a two-by-four snipe that ran around over the glades with some bootleggers and a cattle thief and wrote what he thought was a whale of a story in the yellowest sheet in Miami about the Florida Indian work.[18] He had discovered old Johnny Buster, and had a whacking story about the Florida Indian Service's neglect of him, but he got his name mixed up. I absolutely refused to straighten him out and so he skipped it. But what he had planned to say about this case was as far from facts as all the other items he reported.

Pictures number twenty-nine and thirty show an Indian family that lived in "Blue Field," east of Okeechobee. I do not know of another family that has cost the government more, or that had gone to the dogs so badly. In the early part of my work I took one of the girls to Ft. Pierce for a major operation, and after she got stronger her father and I built a camp for her near Okeechobee, and I bought her food and medicine until they were able to return to this old woods. Sometime later the father found a distillery and drank so much that he died at the camp we built. They burned it to destroy any future visitation of evil on them.

The old mother was going blind, and I took her to Miami for a major operation. This was one Indian I refused to give facts. She wanted to know if anyone had ever died in her room. She was scared so bad, anyhow, that she did not sleep all night, and we knew she would not stay if she knew that people had died there. On the morning after she arrived she said that she had seen white arms reaching down from the ceiling for her all night long. It was the first time she had ever

18. In 1934, the *Miami Daily News* published a thirty-eight page booklet which was a compilation of articles written by staff writer Cecil R. Warren. This series of fifteen articles, printed with accompanying letters to the editor and affidavits by various persons, attempted to paint a picture of governmental indifference and neglect of the Seminole people who were in desperate circumstances during the depression years. Several of the articles were uncomplimentary in their appraisal of Glenn's efforts, and he felt that the series was politically inspired and distorted the real situation. Cecil R. Warren, *Florida's Seminoles* (Miami: *Miami Daily News*, 1934).

29

been alone with white people, or had slept in a white man's house.

The first of these pictures shows the kind of set up they were satisfied to have. They could have built a home like that of Billie Stewart, but they were too indolent. The second picture of the group shows one of the young mothers at her sewing machine as she sits on the ground amid the brush.

I ran all over three counties in an effort to make the father of the oldest half-white child support his baby. He and other boys had joked these girls about being their sweethearts, and had given them all the whiskey they could drink, and had gone their way. The mother of the oldest child had ruined my case by refusing to testify unless we paid her for acting as a witness.

As soon as the next young girl in the family got old enough she let one of this group of boys make believe he was becoming her husband, and she gave birth to this little child that sits beside her.

Billie Stewart came to me for help in connection with both these girls and their brothers. He said that Sam Jones wanted to shoot them, but he did not think they ought to do that. The Indians were made to marry their Indian companions, but I know of no way of making a white man marry one of these women, even if that seemed best. But for five years or more this family got $25 worth of medical service per month. And yet our two-by-four snipe paraded this family as one that had been utterly neglected.

Johnny Osceola, who was one of the prominent Indians of Collier County, was old and crippled with arthritis, and had been placed on government relief for a number of years. He spent his time in the Indian country east of Immokalee, at Miami, and at the Agency. At Miami he layed around one of those commercial Indian villages, and since the owner of the villages made a lot of money out of having him at the camp the owner fed him while he was there. But Johnny was given his groceries each month at Immokalee or Dania during the time that he was away from Miami. It was his son, Charlie Osceola, who had fought the axe-wielding, drunken Indian off of me. Charlie and his brother Robert were both married, and were employed at the Agency from time to time.

At one time, after Johnny had been at the Agency for some weeks, he told me he wanted to go back to Immokalee, and wanted to ride with me on my next trip over there. I loaded him and his family on my car at the first opportunity, and left them in an Indian camp outside of Immokalee. They waited there a few days until some of the Indians came in from the Hendry County reservation after which they planned to go back out to this region.

You can guess how mad I was when I read this two-by-four snipe's story in his yellow sheet on the next day that there was a God-forsaken, old, sick, Indian at Immokalee that the Agency had utterly neglected.

Although I had risked my own health and that of my family when Robert was ill, and Charlie had defended me, and I had given them work and looked after the old father, Charlie came into my office one day, both drunk and mad. He had a pistol in his hand. I said, "What is it, Charlie? Had not you better give me that gun?" He handed me the gun and replied, "Mr. H., he say you lie *ojus*." Mr. H. was our famous fanatic of Ft. My-

30

ers.[19] I suspected that Mr. H. had not planned for Charlie to give the gun to me that way.

This raising hell in the Indian work is a science as fully developed as the science of smoke screening an army or a task force of the navy. The more hell that is created, the more is covered up the motives and character of those who do the raising.

I told you of some of the difficulties that I had with the family at "Blue Field." A young married white boy at Immokalee determined to break down the chastity of two early teenage Indian girls in his region by getting the whole camp drunk. The two girls had been at the Agency only a few days before, and the men in their families had been on the work crew. Old Charlie Dixie, a half-Negro Indian, fought this boy for some time and tried to get the two girls away from him, but he ran Charlie off, and continued to pour whiskey down these two children. They fought him as long as they were conscious.

Our famous fanatic of Fort Myers heard the story first and began raising hell, as usual. He wrote the Senators and the Congressmen, but he failed to see the prosecuting attorney who lived in his own town. When the case was brought before a grand jury the men of the panel embarrassed the girl with their own lustful curiosity, and she refused to answer questions that had no bearing, whatever, on the matter of justice.

I took the case to the federal court in Miami and fought so hard to convict the boy that the judge asked me to go with his probation officer and investigate the whole affair. The officer and I drove back into the Indian country as far as we could, and then walked for some miles through the glades to a Green Corn Dance they were attending. When we arrived the Indians did not want to be disturbed in the first place, and there were some of the more reactionary members of the tribe who believed that it was bad policy to go to the white courts for justice. They had rather bear their wrongs. The girl lay flat on her stomach with her heels kicked up in the air

19. "Mr. H." was probably W. Stanley Hanson, son of Dr. William Hanson who had befriended the Seminoles during the 1880s. He was perhaps the one white man most trusted by the Indians in the first three decades of this century. Hanson was born in Key West in 1883, moved to Fort Myers the next year, and spent the remainder of his life there. He engaged in a number of businesses, but was best known as a hunting guide and Everglades explorer. A charter member of the Seminole Indian Association, founded at Fort Myers in 1913, he served for many years as its unpaid secretary. In that capacity he traveled thousands of miles each year at his own expense promoting the Seminole cause. He and his supporters were of the opinion that governmental efforts to assist the Seminoles were both minimal and ill-directed at best. There were several attempts to have Hanson considered for the post of Indian Agent, but he never was appointed to an official position. Agent Glenn felt that, although Hanson did much good for the Indians, he and his organization were also a divisive influence which undercut governmental efforts to rehabilitate the tribe. Hanson died in Fort Myers on April 4, 1945. *Fort Myers News-Press*, April 5, 1945. *See also* Harry A. Kersey, Jr., "Private Societies and the Maintenance of Seminole Tribal Integrity, 1899–1957," *Florida Historical Quarterly* 56 (January 1978): 311–16.

while we talked to her. No man can make a case when his witness behaves that way. She was not an immodest girl, but she did not understand what it was all about, and wanted to forget it.

The second most sensational case came in the investigation of the death of Jessie Morgan. I told earlier in this story of an Indian who got drunk on rubbing alcohol and was tied up by the women at the Indian Agency. This was Robert Osceola, and the young Indian he blasted with the pipe wrench was Jessie.

Both of these boys one would like a very great deal. I had two other young boys that were tops when they were sober. They were Wilson Tigertail and Johnny Billie. These last two were buddies, and both hunted together and worked together when they were at the Agency. Wilson was the boy who cried over the supposed death of his sister. One day Wilson and Johnny came back from selling some pelts and they were bruised and cut up until they were bloody. I talked to them about it, and they said they had had a gloriously good time from some whiskey they had gotten for their pelts. Johnny, it

seems, was vicious when he got drunk, and wanted to beat up even his buddy.

One Saturday Johnny and Jessie Morgan had been paid off for their week's work at the Agency, and they had gone over to the Big Cypress country between Everglades City and Immokalee. Here they had stopped at a saw mill, and had learned that one of the Negroes at the saw mill had a distillery hid out in the Big Cypress Swamp. That's all they wanted to know. They and Jim Jumper made themselves into a patrol whose purpose it was to find the still. They found it, did not spend any of their money to buy their drinks, but all started the liquor road to this glorious good time. Soon they were fighting, just fighting, they did not know why. Johnny afterwards claimed that Jim slashed Jessie Morgan with his knife. Jessie bled a lot and tried to get back out of the swamp, but fell face down in water a foot deep, and was both too drunk and too weak to get up. Jim was a slick duck. When he was questioned he claimed that Johnny did the knife work. Johnny refused at the time to tell anything. It was Johnny who was arrested and thrown in jail.

The Indians had always tried their own cases, but they could not get to Johnny as long as the sheriff had him. I told them that I did not object to them trying the defendant if they would give him a fair trial. They said they would turn Johnny over to Jessie Morgan's people to be shot. Johnny had the right to hide and the Morgans had the right to hunt. If Johnny could hide better than they could hunt he won the chance to go before the Seminole Council at the next Green Corn Dance and be tried there, and if they condemned him an Indian would be charged with the task of hunting him down and shooting him at some time from an ambush. The strange part of it was that Seminoles so condemned would stick with their tribe and be shot, rather than seeking refuge with other Indians of the nation.

The white hearing in Everglades City was a meeting ground of all the hell raisers in Florida. You know we have lady tyrants as well as gentlemen tyrants. One of the former swore that in her opinion Johnny had not killed Jessie, but she urged the court to let the Indians have him. The attorney said,

"Don't you believe that they would kill him?" She thought so, but she thought they ought to try their own cases. That was good diplomacy. The Indians liked that, and would remember it.

I told the court that in my opinion the courts of the American nation had the only legal jurisdiction in Florida or any other state. That it was legally impossible to hand the case over to the jurisdiction of another form of government. If the court wanted to simply dismiss the case on the basis of insufficient evidence such a course would be legal. To my very great surprise the court said, "You are their Agent. We appoint you as his keeper."

And that was "bad" diplomacy for me. You have never stood for a man's life and you have never experienced that kind of responsibility. Men who have do not take it lightly unless they are murderers themselves. I took Johnny by a lot of Indian camps on my trip back to the Agency, but they were too law abiding to try to take him away from me. I told Johnny that as long as he stayed at the Agency, and stayed sober, I would see that he was not killed. He never drank another drop of liquor while I was there, and his conduct was good. Some of the Indians came to say, "Mr. Glenn, his medicine alright." My successor had a fight with Johnny and ran him off the reservation. He went to Miami, got drunk, beat up Johnny Osceola's daughter, and Johnny Osceola shot him down with a shotgun in one of the commercial camps of Miami. So they got him after all.

Photograph number thirty-one shows Sam Tommie on one of his horses. The Tommie family was one of the prominent families of the tribe.[20] His mother was a woman of more than usual intelligence. She and her boys lived at the Agency, but Sam married a Ft. Pierce Indian, and her people made him live with them. Sam's brother had a grammar school education, and Sam had learned from him how to read and write. In my trips with him through the Indian country I found him as good company as any white man. We stopped one day in a small town and he climbed out of the car and started across the street. He met a small Negro girl who evidently was not accustomed to meeting "real Indians." Her big white eyes rolled up at him and she made every preparation to "clear out" of that place if he noticed her. When Sam returned I told him about the girl, and said, "Such a big and dangerous man as you are ought not to frighten even little Negro girls." Sam understood that I was "kidding him" and laughed over it as much as I did.

This business of buying land for a Semi-

20. The Tommie family has played a prominent role in the modern history of the Seminole Tribe as they adapted to reservation life. Annie Tommie was one of the first Seminoles to move to the Dania Reservation when it opened in 1926. Earlier, her son Tony had been the first Indian student to attend the Fort Lauderdale elementary school for three years, beginning in 1915. Another of her sons, Sam Tommie, became a lay Baptist preacher and was instrumental in getting families to move to the outlying reservations during the 1930s. Sam's son, Howard Tommie, has served several terms as the elected chairman of the Seminole Tribal Council, and was also president of the United Southeastern Tribes, which represents many federally recognized tribes in the eastern United States. Bill McGoun, *A Biographic History of Broward County* (Miami: *The Miami Herald,* 1972), pp. 47–48.

31

nole home or homes is a most difficult task, and Sam and Mr. King and some of the other Indians worked on it a great deal. When this picture was taken Sam and I were discussing this problem. Mr. Nash had recommended that the Agency be located in Collier County. There are more Indians in that county than in all of the other counties of the state. But there are no stock range lands, except in the Immokalee country and to the east of that town, in the whole Indian-occupied part of the county. The best hunting is still here, and it is improbable that they will give up hunting as long as they can find game. Tomato growing is a gold mine to white farmers, but who would gamble on getting Indians to grow such crops? Land prices are another consideration. The owner of this Collier County land had paid about six dollars per acre for it. We set up a tract of four sections of land about fifteen miles north of the city of Everglades. This was the highest and driest spot south of the Big Cypress Swamp. Some of the land was sold to a white farmer for fifty dollars per acre. I got an option on the four sections for six dollars per acre, and got the state forest division to loan me an appraiser to go over it. He did about two weeks of jungle work and came out with an appraised value of twenty-five dollars per acre. Dr. Hartmann was dissatisfied with this report and sent his own appraiser down. Since he proposed to pay for the land from his unit of the government, I was happy to have him go over it again. He got a report of about six dollars per acre.

Mr. Ernest F. Coe, sponsor of the Everglades National Park, wanted the Seminoles located in a strip of land running across the northern line of the Park. We then set up about a hundred thousand acres for purchase in Collier County, and Mr. Copeland got an option on it for me at six dollars per acre. He did not want it sold at all. A lot of it was not worth anything but some of it had thirty or forty dollars per acre of timber on it. He wanted to help me in my program so badly, however, that he said, "The large tract in this proposed reservation which we do not own belongs to a Mr. X in Ft. Myers. I believe you could get it for fifty cents per acre."

I wrote Mr. X that I would take an option on this land if I could get it for fifty cents per acre. He gave it to me. To justify this six dollar per acre purchase after I had gotten the fifty cents per acre option was impossible. Neither I nor Copeland had foreseen that. It is probable that a lot of this land-buying proposal was ballyhoo so far as the brass hats in Washington were concerned. Hartmann thought so and told me that "they" were making a monkey out of me. The Indians had a hundred thousand acre tract in the lower Everglades National Park area that the state had given the Seminoles "if they would live on it." It was utterly worthless except for hunting. The Park people wanted it, and wanted the state to swap it for a tract of land north of the Tamiami Trail. The state land commission agreed to make the exchange if the Indian Office would buy additional lands itself. These projects that I set up, after more labor than anyone knows except myself, were the kind of ballyhoo that would get the deal through from the state.

Hartmann said his department would go all the way with me on the purchase of the Indian Prairie Reservation. He and I got the project in proper form and included in it the purchase of 35,000 acres, and its improvement for an Indian population. I flatly refused to accept the project unless it was given to the Seminoles. So it was made as a grant, and Tugwell's office approved it.[21] But my bunch of brass hats threw it out of the window. Hartmann was so sick about it that he gave me a copy of the letter that he had had from Tugwell's office, and lost his job over it, or some other such thing.

I then dovetailed my plans with those of a group of army engineers who were building a great dam about Lake Okeechobee to safeguard the farming area from floods during a hurricane. There were 70,000 acres of this number one pasture land on the northwest shore of the lake that could not be included in the safety zone by these engineers. Since the white farmers wanted to live on the lake shore and farm such land as could be irrigated from the lake they could no longer make use of this region. But because the Indians would raise stock and would never think of putting their homes in such a danger spot as that lake shore it could be used by them. I wrote the proposal to Senator [Duncan U.] Fletcher and he answered that it was the best solution of that whole matter that he could think of, and he said he would gladly introduce a bill in Congress for the purchase of this 70,000 acre tract.

A few days later I had a letter from him saying he had discussed the matter with my brass hats, and that they had thrown it out the window. I called on the state land commissioner and asked him to use his trading power with the Indian Office to get the Seminoles at least one tract of good land.

This had all happened in spite of the fact that I had had Collier and Ickes down at Florida, and they had both committed their departments to buy the Indians a home.[22] The Indians were a squatter population, and had

21. Rexford G. Tugwell, a leading advocate of scientific planning for agricultural land use, served as Undersecretary of Agriculture to Henry Wallace. In 1935, as part of a general reorganization of New Deal programs, Tugwell was made head of the newly created Resettlement Administration. At the request of John Collier, Tugwell agreed to allow Indians to use the Resettlement Administration's program of crop loans, drought relief, and subsistence grants. By 1936 this assistance had been extended to other self-help projects with special emphasis on creating subsistence homestead communities. Philp, *John Collier's Crusade,* pp. 125–26.

22. In 1935, Secretary of the Interior Harold Ickes, his wife Anna, and their son Raymond, accompanied by Commissioner John Collier, visited the Seminole Indians of Florida. The purpose of the visit, as Collier viewed it, was "to conclude a kind of treaty of peace between the United States government and the Seminoles, and to bring them into our Indian efforts." After visiting various Indian camps in the region, the Collier-Ickes party met with an unofficial delegation of Seminoles in West Palm Beach during a civic celebration, and received their petition requesting that the federal authorities purchase certain parcels of land and provide cash annuities. Although Secretary Ickes made no specific guarantees to purchase the lands requested, he did state that the Seminoles should have more land of their own and pledged greater federal efforts in that direction. Apparently Agent Glenn and some of the Indians took this as a specific commitment to direct and immediate action. John Collier, *From Every Zenith* (Denver: Sage Books, 1963), pp. 289–90; Bureau of Indian Affairs, *Annual Report, Narrative Section, 1935, Seminole Agency, Dania, Florida,* pp. 7–9; August Burghard, "Seminole Indians Ask Uncle Sam for New Deal," *Fort Lauderdale Daily News,* March 21, 1935.

no legal right on any land except such as had been previously bought. These former tracts were sixteen in number and were largely worthless.

After I was separated from the Florida work two tracts were bought. I know the Indian Prairie Reservation will pay off in the years to come. I do not know anything about the other tract.

Reading from left to right the men in photograph number thirty-two are Mr. [Charles] Roblin of the Indian Land Office in Washington; Mr. [Lewis] Thorp, the sheriff of Collier County; and Mr. D. Graham Copeland, the manager of the Barron G. Collier interests in Florida. Mr. Roblin is a man of genuine integrity, and had a lot to do with the final purchase of the Florida lands, unless he was kicked out of the Washington Office. They were "booting" him severely when he was last in Florida.

The picture was made some ten or twelve miles north of the Tamiami Trail at the eastern end of Collier County. This is a very small spot of the land that Mr. Ernest F. Coe wanted for the Seminoles. It is the region north of the north line of the Everglades National Park. Mr. Copeland has found the corner post of a section survey and is fastening a paper to it. The land was surveyed about a half-century ago, and was marked by fat pine stalks. Many of these have rotted and so it is an event to discover one.

If you will examine the ground here you will discover that it is covered with water plants and that it is almost bare. There is a marl soil that is usually two or three inches deep. Rock projects up through it to sweet sunlight. We took Mr. Thorp along because his truck was about the only thing that could get through and he was one of the few who knew how to get through. We were bumping along over rocks as large as a man's body and Thorp hit one just a little too hard. The car heaved over to its side, and our host, Mr. Copeland, slid out of it, and landed in a most undignified heap on a solid rock surface.

This is the dry season or we could never go in there. There is some timber as can be seen, and wherever there is pine the land is "high." Many thousands of acres of this country are covered with a dwarf cypress that is six or eight feet high and from two to three inches in diameter.

If this land were drained, and not over drained, and if it were cleared and sodded to grass it would be valuable pasture land, but that would cost a great deal of money. I think there has been some oil discovered in part of Collier County land like this. For all the use that can be made of it in its present condition the Indians have that without buying it. The timber will be cut, and some of it may be farmed, but this is largely a white man's job. In the meantime the Seminoles can roam over it for weeks, months and even years and never so much as see a white man.

Picture number thirty-three shows the pasture lands in the region around Lake Okeechobee. Contrast this growth of grass with that shown in the other picture and you will know why Dr. Hartmann and I finally took our risk with the Indian Prairie Reservation lands rather than the Collier County land. The Collier County Indians are located on the Tamiami Trail and in the east end of the county. The latter group can be reached by the road that runs south from Clewiston. Those on the highway would be better off if they were induced to find a home back up at Guava Camp or farther north.

There is a group of Dade County Indians that would be a long way from Clewiston, but surely not as far as they are from Ft. Myers. They accept only medical service from the government. They are an energetic group, and some of them manage to make good money out of acting as the "middle man" between the rest of the Indians and the white trader. William McKinley Osceola makes about several hundred dollars per month during the trapping season by organizing the Indians into hunting patrols, and "spotting" these several patrols at the right time and place for getting the most pelts. He hauls a group and their supplies in his car to a good canal bank, and gives them a week or two weeks to get the otter or raccoon there. He returns, takes them into town, buys their pelts, and takes them to another well-stocked lake or stream.

His white jobber in pelts furnishes him capital, and ships the hides to the market. So long as this lasts this is good organization, and brings a good income for all concerned.

But it is a very heavy raid on the wildlife of South Florida. William is very certain that the white man is to obey the white man's law and the Indian the Indian "game law." If he can use the white man's law to close the season to white hunting it will help him in his well-paying industry. But even then this kind of organization will destroy all wildlife even if no one hunted but the Indian.[23]

I still have a picture of Old Charlie Tigertail. He was one of those gracious old men who made you happy to know him. He was a direct descendent of the Chief Tigertail. I asked him one day if he thought that the white man killed all of the game. He said,

23. Glenn was correct in noting the destructive effect of white overhunting in the region. Before the turn of the century white hunters had entered the Everglades in great numbers, seeking the bird plumes, alligator hides, and otter pelts prized by the international fashion industry. Bands of "plumers" systematically shot up entire rookeries during nesting season, when the plumage was at its most brilliant, and cared little whether hatchlings survived the carnage. Similarly, hunters using high-speed boats and battery-powered

"White man hunt too much—Indian hunt too much." Translated he meant that both were to blame for the destruction of the wild life of that region—the Indian as much as the white man. I thought he was a most generous-minded man.

Perhaps you would want to see some of the cattle that the Indian Prairie range was feeding. They are shown in photograph number thirty-four. Mr. Nash had a story of a cattle buyer who lived in Chicago, and who wired a ranchman in Florida for 500 cattle that weight 1500 pounds each. The ranchman wired back, "Sorry, I have no cattle in the fifteen hundred pound weight bracket, but I

lights dominated alligator hunting; they also took thousands of otter pelts with their superior traps. Only the collapse of the market for these goods around the time of World War I gave the Everglades wildlife a reprieve until the late 1920s. By the 1930s the Seminoles had become a very minor factor in the limited pelt and hide trade in Florida. Harry A. Kersey, Jr., *Pelts, Plumes and Hides: White Traders Among the Seminole Indians, 1870–1930* (Gainesville: University Presses of Florida, 1975).

32

33

will gladly ship you 1500 cattle that will weigh 500 each."

The native stock of Florida are small and, since the stockman depends upon the native grasses to support his animals the year around, and because the animals are eaten up with ticks and mosquitoes, they have to be tough or die. However, it will be seen that the cattle in this picture are in good condition, and range in weight up to about a thousand pounds each. Several million of these native cattle roam over the pine woods and higher prairies of the state. The men who own them do not own or lease the lands on which they range, but claim an indisputable title to them. Feuds break out between the owners of different herds, and men are killed as a result of these feuds. These gun battles develop, of course, over the possession of the better range lands. I was told that four men had been killed in the fight over the use of the grass lands on this Indian Prairie country.

I once owned an automobile that the garagemen described to me as "just a hard luck car." It was always in the repair shop. I do not know of any people on earth who have

been victimized more outrageously than the Indian population of the United States. They are victimized both by the hell raisers and by the uplifters. And of all the hard luck that has been piled on any of the tribes I think the Seminoles of Florida have been buried the deepest in this mountain of misfortune.

I have already told you how they, themselves, were refugees from the power, cunning, and resourcefulness of the United States armed forces. But the Everglades country was a hideout for the refugees of another American war, and these refugees were not superlative patriots but yellow-spined slackers who fled the Union Army in the Civil War. They escaped military service, but jungle life often leads to barbarism. The "roaring West" is featured in story as a "pistol-packing people," but the type of semi-pirate which even now is to be found on the lower Florida Keys is not so widely known. A lady who owned the theater in Arcadia told me that some of these "wild men" used to bring their guns to her show, and when the drama waxed hot they would join in the battle against the villain and as a result would shoot her screen full of holes.

A Mr. C. G. McKinney,[24] who was the postmaster of Chokoloskee and who was the only man on the Island who was not engaged

24. Charles G. McKinney (1847–1926), born in Georgia, moved with his family to Florida in 1854. As a young Confederate soldier during the Civil War he served in the command of Capt. F. A. Hendry (for whom Hendry County, Fla., is named). Following the war McKinney engaged in farming and operated a saw mill in North Florida, but a near-fatal bout with pneumonia led him to move to the southern end of the peninsula. In 1886 he settled on Turner River and farmed for two years with R. B. Turner. His next move was to Chokoloskee Island, where he opened a general store and became postmaster in 1891. Early in this century he began writing the local island news for the *American Eagle* newspaper, published in Estero, Fla. His humorous accounts of bootleggers, preachers, Indians, and the social life of the island were reprinted by other newspapers throughout the state from time to time. McKinney continued writing these columns until his death in 1926. Charlton W. Tebeau, *The Story of the Chokoloskee Bay Country* (Miami: n.p., 1955), pp. 19–26.

34

in some phase of getting whiskey from Cuba to the United States or selling it after it had been smuggled in, might well be described as a "swamp humorist." He has succeeded in giving the best candid camera picture of life among these Island people. On July 2, 1924, he writes, "Charlie Tigertail was here this week. He brought some bananas and sugar cane up from his farm to sell to us. Fishing is not very good. Mullet is scarce and trout a little more so." On August 20, 1924, he writes, "We have had no rain, but we have had some Indians this week. No booze and no preaching. We read in the paper of 'low bush lightning' (whiskey) striking 200 persons or more right in the city of Washington, and how the big officials were scandalized. Can't see how that could be unless they were around and smelled the breath of those that were struck by the lightning. ... Fishing is better this week. Mullet is more plentiful but the trout refuses to take the hook."

On the 9th of October he wrote, "We have had this week some very strange evidence last Sunday of low bush lightning. Some of the disciples (church members) had the stuff that looked red and we supposed that it was low bush goods. They asked us to take a nip but we had to decline. ... We have plenty of bootleggers around and all are doing well. Fishing is good."

Again on September 18, 1924, "A lot of rain yesterday. Fishing is not very good. We have a new school teacher, came in this week. She was a little late but reached us all the same. We have had some symptoms of low bush lightning this week. Nothing very serious. We have had a few Indians. Our preacher is to pay us a visit again tomorrow. He will have time to tell them what will become of them in the wind-up if they don't be good."

November 6, 1924, "Fishing is good. Bootlegging is good. Moonshining on the draw back, the Satan Angels (drunkards) seem to like the imported stuff. ... We have no preacher yet but the folks is getting on about as well as ever. ... We have no school either; we don't see or hear any prospects of anyone coming to hold the school down."

December 11, 1924, "We have some signs of low bush lightning this week and some Indians under the influence of it, and some others just the same. We have decided that there is nothing in the prohibition game as long as so many officers can be bought off with from one to a few bottles or cases of booze. ... If the good Lord had set a bottle of booze in the corner of the Garden of Eden and told Adam to let it alone, Adam could not sleep at night but he would have crawled out there and got a corkscrew and pulled the cork and filled up his tank, and went back and pulled old Eve from the bed and beat her up . ... We have a few swamp angels (mosquitoes) on the Island now and suppose they have come to enjoy the Christmas with us. Nearly all the men folks have gone from the Island, hunting coons and otters and some other pursuits to gather in the almighty dollar with which to buy grits. We have no preacher and no school teacher yet."

On the first of the next year he reports, "We have had preaching all week . ... The hunters, both Indian and whites, are bringing in a big lot of coon skins and some others . ... We see from the news that there are lots of booze ships being captured from foreign ports (from Cuba) with big cargoes of the Devil's goods."

Back in June of the year he writes, "We have quite a lot of the swamp angels yet but they don't seem to be as crazy as they were last week but they are pretty busy. We have a few Indians, all sober. We have no booze this week. Fishing is very good. We expected the schooner *Newport* this week from Key West. We hope she will be in next week. It is likely that she will run on the try weekly schedule (try one week and come the next)."

This is the type of white community into which the Seminole came to do his trading, and these people, about whom Mr. Mc-Kinney writes, were his neighbors and "friends." They were not so much hell raisers as a muck and mire that sucked under the character of both the individual Indian and the whole social body of the tribe. Charlie Tigertail, whom I have commended, used some of this sugar cane not to sell to Mr. McKinney, but to make this low bush lightning. That he did is tragic, but the evil grew from his environment.

But I have mentioned this uplifter oppression that has devastated both the Seminole and all other tribes. In an editorial back in 1929 I wrote, "A wowser is a professionalized uplifter who, lacking the insight and moral discrimination of the genuine prophet, is nevertheless possessed with the reform complex. He occasionally endeavors to reform his superiors and frequently tries to uplift his equals. His standards are both stereotyped and provincial and more likely are concerned with differences in social customs than with moral issues. The type of dress or the cut of the hair are matters upon which he is ready to call out the loyal legions of his god, and against which he directs his crusading armies. He puts his trust in the sword rather than moral persuasion."

My lady tyrant, whom I have already mentioned, and whom I met a number of years later, belongs to this class of uplifter. But I have since discovered two other types. The first of these we shall call the clock-punching uplifter. At eight in the morning she punches the clock of her employee and begins an eight hour grind of this business of uplifting. She then punches the clock again and returns to a life in another sphere altogether. For more than one century the Indian Service has "hounded" the tribes of the United States with this type of employee.

My final type is the hobbiest uplifter. These are usually wealthy people who become bored with a life of indolence. They have to have a hobby or go crazy. They make a hobby of the pageantry of Indian life and custom, and begin to up or down lift these people as per whichever course promotes the ends of their hobby.

The Indians and I drew such a woman from Miami. She had a lovely home, wealth, and time to waste. She discovered that she was a sensation in the social circles of her city when she donned an Indian woman's dress and gave a half-baked harangue about letting the Indian be an Indian.

Let me say another thing. A great deal has been discovered about these "mental cases" that develop among soldiers in modern warfare. These mental cases are individuals. But a whole community or even a nation may become obsessed with this psychological happening when it is subjected to an abnormal condition. Such an abnormal condition exists in the "wide open" tourist towns of Florida. The diagnosis of the public mind of Miami will show that it is a "mental case." It is not the only town in Florida that has this mental disease. This condition is the gravest threat that can endanger the democratic way of life. Because, under these circumstances, fanatics are elevated to office.

Miami elevated our Miami hobbiest uplifter to a position which made it imperative that I collaborate with her. She used this fact to discover what tracts of land I wanted for the Indians after which she moved heaven and earth to keep me from getting them.

In the meantime the public mind of the nation as a whole had developed this "slap-happy" complex. After suffering the torture of a war we were plunged into a panic, and were confronted with a more destructive war. Men in Washington were saying, "Education has not saved us from all of this, and we do not think it will serve the welfare of the Seminoles." The whole concept of human progress was being thrown into the ash can, and men who were ready to break with these old tenets were entrusted with the formulation of public policy. The directive which I heard in the administrative councils of my Washington office amounted to some-

thing like this: "Get results first and justify the ethics of your policy afterwards."

The Indian Office had drawn a large element of this hobbiest uplifter school of reform, and was most receptive to my sensation of Miami social circles. Suppose I had been trying to get you in school, or a place to work, or under treatment by a doctor or in the hospital, and suppose that your whole social being was enmeshed in such powerful and conflicting dynamics; do you think that anyone could say that you were born "with a silver spoon in your mouth" or that great good fortune had been handed to you?

We have fought a war over our Negro population, but with all the suffering that that race has endured it has a more advantageous position in America than the Indian race now has, throttled as it is with Washington brass hats and too many friends. For that the capital of the world's greatest republic should be founded upon such a thoroughgoing feudalistic social organization as is Washington is the greatest travesty of all political history. God help any people whose most intimate, immediate, and individual interests must be administered from such a center. For the feu-

dalist is so constituted that when he is not licking the boots of somebody he is making someone lick his boots.

These are some of the social and civil problems that dog these "primitive children of the forest."

I have told you that after the close of the Seminole Wars, and during the period when patrols of the United States Army were scouting through the Everglades to capture each and every member of the tribe, the several family groups discovered a hideout on the west shore line of what was then Lake Okeechobee. This is now the eastern end of Collier and Hendry counties. We have shown you the home of Billie Stewart. I have a fine group of pictures on some of the homes of these east Collier County Indians. I want to take you through these pictures to visit some of their camps.

The first camp that we shall visit is Californee, as you may see in picture number thirty-five. At the little town of Immokalee you leave behind this big old United States as you know it, and plunge out into the kind of world that faced DeSoto, LaSalle, Clark

35

and Daniel Boone. There are automobile tracks that lead in the general direction in which you are going, but all landmarks look alike, and these car tracks branch off both to the right and the left hand. You recall in the story of the three bears, one pot of soup was too hot and another was too cold but the third was just right. In picking out your road in the glades one will be too wet, and because the ground is covered with a slime you will have no traction and the rear wheels will spin. Another is too dry, and the car will bury itself in loose, white sand. But there is almost always a third that is neither too wet nor too dry, but just right if you can find it. And that is the reason these automobile tracks spread all over the country before you. I have never been lost in this section but once. At the request from a fellow worker from Washington, I tried to find my road at night time. We arrived not at the house on the Hendry County Reservation, but at an abandoned Indian camp a few miles north of it. We back tracked about twenty miles, altogether, and arrived at our destination at about midnight.

But Californee is another fifteen or twenty miles east and south of this place. This is one of the most beautiful Indian homes that I have ever known. Here lived Billy Fewl[25] and his son-in-law, Wilson Cypress. Billy was perhaps a hundred years old when I first visited him. He had been a resourceful man, and had led his people during a most difficult period of readjustment, and was one of the older men who had the respect of this whole group. George W. Storter, one of those sturdy pioneers who have made this great nation possible, says that shortly after he located at the place that is now known as Everglades City he made an expedition up into the region to the north. He was both scouting and hunting, but he found a lone Indian in a canoe, and waited to meet him and talk with him. This was young Billy Fewl, who, himself, was scouting down near the coast in an effort to find a market where his people could sell their goods and purchase needed supplies. Mr. Storter had set up a store for the white people along the coast, but told Billy that he would trade with the Indians, and assured him that he would be as honest with them as he was with all his neighbors. This was the beginning of a friendship that is not only a credit to the best of a very fine citizenship in Florida, but to the best manhood of both the Indian and white races.

One has to see much of this glades country to know how hostile it is to life in a desolate land. The Rev. Alexander Linn[26] and I visited this home in 1928 for the first

25. Billy Fewl (also commonly spelled Fewell) was one of the best known Seminoles of his day. A Mikasuki-speaker from the Big Cypress Swamp region, he was the brother of Billy Conapatchee, the first Seminole known to have attended school (while living with the Hendry family of Fort Myers during the 1870s). Billy Fewell received his nickname "Key West Billy" for having ostensibly poled his canoe to that island city at one time. Clay MacCauley, "The Seminole Indians of Florida," in *5th Annual Report, 1883–1884*, Smithsonian Institution, Bureau of American Ethnology (Washington: Government Printing Office, 1887), p. 485.

26. Alexander Linn was a Presbyterian minister who served as a Sunday-school missionary in Florida. He worked among the Seminoles and

time. Billy showed us his guns, and his knives, and talked with us about the deer he had killed with this gun, and the bear he had killed with another. He was a gracious host, and at meal time shared some of his daughter's biscuits. The home is built on a high spot of land and is surrounded with guava and banana trees. He wanted us to sleep on one of these catch-all tables that is part of every Indian home. One feels just a whole lot of loneliness settle down on him as night comes over him and he and his white companion close their eyes for sleep, and try to forget such strange surroundings. It had been very hot through the day, for the glades were dry, and the rock formation absorbed the sun's rays and cooked the lower atmosphere

▼▼▼▼▼▼▼▼▼▼▼▼▼▼▼▼▼▼▼▼▼▼▼▼▼▼▼▼▼▼▼▼▼▼▼▼▼

had hoped for the appointment as Indian Agent which Glenn received. Although they were good friends, Glenn believed that Linn thought he had the inside track because he was a Republican and Glenn was a Democrat. "Interview with Dr. James L. Glenn, January 12, 1978," tape recording, University of Florida Indian Oral History Archives, Florida State Museum, Gainesville.

with heat. But night brought a cool breeze from the distant Atlantic, and the Indian people in the home gathered about their campfire and laughed and talked until almost midnight.

Sleep came to us when the stars were glowing in all their glory, and all animal life was hushed in silence. In fact, I had no notion that there were any animals to be seen or heard in the whole region, but at dawn Billy Fewl's old rooster slapped his wings and sang his crude song of a new day. As my mind pushed sleep aside I was completely astonished to discover that the whole region was ringing with the music of birds, some of which I had never heard before.

Photograph number thirty-six shows Billy Fewl in his "garden." Aside from the hat, he wears the old dress of the Seminole man. It is easy to misunderstand the folk stories of other races, because we think they really believe them. Billy told us a story about this garden, which he did not believe any more than we believe our stories of good or ill luck. He said that the Indians say that if, after you cut the brush away, dig up, and

fence a plot of land like this for a garden, a young Indian maiden in her birthday dress passes through it in the wee hours of the night the plot will be blessed with rich ground and plenty of corn, pumpkins, and other products.

There is a short period through the year in Florida that the stock flies flourish like the locust of Egypt. Picture number thirty-seven shows some of the few cows which Billy Fewl and his son-in-law owned. They came into the yard and about the campfire because the Indian men built a fire with much smoke and this smoke ran the flies away from them. Some of the logs of the fire can be seen under the body of the cow, and the smoke is seen in the attic of this Indian kitchen. Billy Fewl has on another suit of clothes, and Wilson has the famous Seminole shirt and a pair of trousers that he has bought from a store. Billy's cap is the only one of its kind that I have seen them wear.

Linn and I lost the oil in the crank case of our car and had no way to get back to our own people unless we found some oil in an Indian household. You will see the old model-T at the left of Billy Fewl's arm. He was not using this car, and was good enough to sell us the oil in it. It was a lifesaver to us.

In photograph number thirty-eight, you see one of the women at this camp grinding her corn with a small grist mill. You recall that in another picture we saw the mortar and pestle with which they pounded some of their corn into grits or corn meal. Here, too, is the old rooster and one or two hens. They hope that this woman will drop some corn and they can get it. A steel trap is shown hanging from the catch-all platform.

Earlier in this story I told you about the help that these husbands gave their wives when cooking time came. Photograph number thirty-nine shows Wilson Cypress and his wife working together to prepare the breakfast. She has a pot of sofkee on the fire and he is putting some coffee on it.

The next two pictures were taken here and at Guava camp. Photograph number forty shows the water supply for these families. This water is not polluted, but a small open hole like this can catch grasshoppers, a lot of dust, and other things that do not improve its sanitation. It is baked by the hot Florida sun and is warm. The glades water itself, for the

36

37

most part, is said to be as pure as the water supply of any large city. But the water, like the game, often went far away, and the women had to carry it for perhaps a half mile. Picture number forty-one shows the well that several of us managed to drive at Guava Camp. Driving this pipe with a sledge hammer through ten or fifteen feet of this rock was enough to get the best of any man. The Seminole who has hold of the pump is Whitney Cypress, the brother of Wilson. The other fellow is Jim Gopher, a Cow Creek Indian,[27] who made his home with us at the Agency. Jim went with me to help me run the hammer. Whitney said he did not want the well, but I could put it down if I wanted to. The family did not use the pump until the dry weather made them, and after they got used to it they wanted it very much.

▼▼▼▼▼▼▼▼▼▼▼▼▼▼▼▼▼▼▼▼▼▼▼▼▼▼▼

27. "Cow Creek Indians" was the term commonly used in referring to those Muskogee-speaking Seminoles living to the north of Lake Okeechobee. The name was derived from the stream where Clay MacCauley first located this band in 1880. MacCauley, "The Seminole Indians of Florida," pp. 508–509.

38

39

I should say that Guava camp was a few miles north of Californee, and was within a hundred yards of the old shore line of Lake Okeechobee. From this point the Indians left by canoe to pole their way across this whole muck country to the east coastline of Florida.

It was here also that the first and perhaps the only all-Indian trading post was established in the years which are now past. A Brown family[28] moved out here, built a store, bought the harvest of wildlife which the Seminoles gathered from the Everglades, and freighted in the merchandise that their Indian customers wanted. As I have worn myself to exhaustion to get through this region I have often wondered who was entitled to the most sympathy, the Seminoles who, after their war, were being hunted down by our soldiers, or the men who were doing the hunting. The Brown family must have earned whatever money they may have made out of this trading post, for freighting goods across the Everglades is most difficult. I have heard one of the engineers who worked on the Tamiami Trail say that he and a crew of men and a yoke of oxen have worked a whole day in transporting a drum of gasoline a mile up to his forward machinery.

But not even this hard work justified the Browns in their traffic in whiskey with the Seminoles. For this post was not only a mercantile establishment, it was a saloon. I have heard Mrs. Brown say that if she were able to recall the past and relive it, she would never, never sell these members of a child race this commodity because of its destructive effects on them.

Photographs forty-two and forty-three are pictures taken at the home of another one of Billy Fewl's neighbors. This one is located several miles south of Californee. As we drive eastward the cypress sloughs are left behind, and there is a prairie region along this old shore line of the lake. Here is a high spot. Two palm trees and two oaks stand out like lone sentinels in a boundless world. The hut to the right of the two palms is the kitchen, and the others are for sleeping or eating.

In the beginning of this story I told you of what motherhood was and what it had to endure in this world of wastelands. Photograph number forty-three is my best story of young Seminole womanhood. Do you notice the tension on those fingers of the hand that is exposed? The camera does not tell the whole story of her modesty but Rev. Linn and I knew that she was a young lady, in the same category as our own daughters. Her love of beauty is shown in this drama of color in her clothes, in the mass of beads about her neck, and in this multicolored hair net. She is bare-

28. W. H. "Bill" Brown was an Englishman who began trading with the Indians of the Big Cypress Swamp region during the late 1880s. Initially, he and his family drove an ox team and wagon loaded with trade goods from Fort Myers to the Indian hunting grounds. Later, he moved to the settlement of Immokalee and opened a general store and trading post. By the turn of the century the Browns had moved again, this time deep into the Big Cypress Swamp, where they established a trading post known as Boat Landing. There the Seminoles could pole their canoes directly to the storefront to trade. In 1908 Brown sold his store to the Episcopal Church, which converted it to a medical mission station. Kersey, *Pelts, Plumes and Hides,* pp. 58–72.

40

41

42

footed but her feet are clothed with her dress. She is about fifteen years old, and romance means just as much to her as it does to any girl of any other race.

When spring comes she will go with her father and mother to the Green Corn Dance, and she will meet and visit with a number of young Indian boys who live far away in other hunting grounds. Her pleasure with this one or the other will be shown by her laughter, the light in her eyes, the swift motion of her body, and her interest in her conversation with him. The two will find the place and the time to talk to each other, or to be together in the group games at the festival, or to eat at the same table. She will play the marvelous drama of "sweetheart" with the same beauty and appeal that young womanhood has known everywhere and at all time. But that drama will never be climaxed with a kiss, for she and her sweetheart shudder at the thought of a saliva-coated lip. They will show their love for one another more by deeds and less by words or other expression. The implacable law of human conventions may turn the Romeo-Juliet of their lives into tragedy. These old family clans mark off, certain

43

young men from her list of possible companions. A few Seminoles cannot marry at all, for tribal law forbids it.[29]

As with other races the parents are to be consulted, and respect for the father or the mother is a very strong force in this social set-up. If there are no conventions that stand in the way, after the two sets of parents discover that these two young people are in love they make up their minds about the matter and discuss these opinions with each other. If they disapprove they try to break up the romance, but if there is no objection the young

29. Glenn's reference here apparently is to a very small number of Seminole-Negro mixed bloods who, although they lived peacefully among the tribe, were forbidden to marry within it. There was no reported Seminole counterpart of the "berdache" found among some other Indian tribes. The berdache was an effeminate male who adopted women's clothing and assumed the woman's role. Such men were usually not scorned but rather regarded with pity and a degree of awe as being victims of conditions beyond their control. Among the tribes of the northern plains they were eligible to join the women's societies.

man "courts" her as any other young man. He gives her his things, and she is as happy to eat a deer that he has killed as a white high-school girl is delighted to wear the sweater that her sweetheart won on the gridiron.

If she and her sweetheart continue to love each other and to find happiness together, the parents of each, finally, make up their minds that they want them to marry. A day is appointed. To the white man, of all the possible disappointments this romance is climaxed with just that. No tribe in all the world loves pageantry more than the Indian, and the Seminole has created the most colorful of any of the Indian tribes. But this marriage—this crowning hour of the greatest of all human drama—this wedding day is wholly without pageantry. All day she watches the trails that lead to her home, and all day she hopes for sundown, and is eager lest he might not come. But he does at sundown, and do they run and kiss or does the medicine man invoke an undying pledge from one to the other? Nothing like that at all. She must tell him she is happy he has come, but he just comes to her camp and begins to live

there ever afterward. His entrance into the camp at sundown on the appointed day concludes the contract.

When her first child comes and looks to her for the things which only a mother can give, she will have those romantic little stories for it that mean so much to childhood—stories not unlike the delightful little child romance of Snow White. Birds in the richest colors of blue, white and scarlet, and gifted with the happiest of songs, the most accommodating and helpful squirrels, cunning and carefree bunnies, and lovely and graceful fawns will move like a pageantry of mirth and sunshine through these romances.

She will tell him of a greater and better peninsula lands than South Florida, where the crane, the curlew, the deer and the otter afford a life filled with both greater prosperity and a more majestic movement of drama. Here rules the greatest of all Big Chiefs, and here too are dancing and song.

But discipline, stern and ugly, highlights this poetry of the child's life. Even before he has learned to walk, social custom will appoint an agent who will take him in his arms, and lash his naked back and legs with the point of a needle. At this letting of blood he will at first tremble with fear and pain, and he will scream with all his might, but this weakness must be overcome.

For to reach this better Seminole homeland he must have endurance. There are swamps and sloughs, so filled with alligators and dangerous animals that they are more hazardous than any in South Florida, which must be crossed in this road that leads to it. His gun and other camping equipment will be buried with him at death, and after three days the living part of him will get up, will face the east, and begin this journey. Because the white man did not have his gun with him when he starts on this trek, the Indian will again become the ruling class and will be the masters of this new world. The Indian way of life will dominate it.

But in the immediate present he lives in a world of both good and evil powers and forces. A medicine man may pronounce a fateful curse on anyone and he will surely die. One evening I took a little child who had died in the Jackson Memorial Hospital of Miami back to his people and said, "Horace is dead. Don't you want to see him?" A member of the family answered, "No! We don't want to die. You take him, bury him."

When a child is born in an Indian home the mother must leave her house and her bedroom and hide somewhere in the palmetto or brush, and there with a bed made of palmetto leaves on the ground give her baby into the arms of a midwife. The father cannot see his child for a period of several days, and the mother and child must not come back into the Seminole house until the danger of death has passed. For if an Indian dies in one of these bedrooms, the whole establishment must be burned.

I thought Jim Gopher lived in a world much like that of other people about me. I asked him to go with me to the home of a sick Cow Creek Indian. These palm hammocks were all alike and it was almost impossible to find a camp unless one had been there before. When we reached this region it began to grow dark and Jimmy became restless and fearful. What if this sick man had died, and I was leading him into such an evil place? He would not be able to see what had taken place in the camp before he reached it.

Although he could have gone to that camp with his eyes closed, almost, he said, "I think so we no find him." And we did "no find him." There was nothing to do but to wait until morning to reach the ill boy.

But their own unique forms of religious rituals could, in some measure, protect him from the evils of this unseen world. Whatever that protection was it was called "medicine." A murderer had had evil powers in his blood, which were removed only by execution. Perhaps a very few men had medicine powerful enough to take it out. Theft, adultery and the most of the other crimes forbidden in the decalog were gotten rid of through execution. George Storter says that when a certain young Indian stole some of his merchandise, and he proved to the chief this fact, the chief brought him the offender and said, "Here, you take him and kill him."

Fortunately their "medicine" was not so feeble in the fight with the demon disease. I have mentioned Annie Tommie, that grand old Indian woman at the Agency. Her grandchild developed an attack of severe cold. Our doctor thought it might be pneumonia. He instructed me to impress on Annie and her people the absolute need of nursing the child with great care. But my talk to them only made them afraid to trust the doctor, and so Annie moved in on the case. When I visited her she had a tin can half full of some clear liquid, and was stirring it with the stem of a water lily. I said, "Annie, get that course of treatment of yours over with and get back on the doctor's medicine. Baby die." She said, "Old Indian, long time ago, show me how to fix them." She was hurt that I had no more respect for her knowledge of medicine. In this case Annie was right. The child got well on Annie's medicine. At other times the proposed remedy was more dangerous than the disease. But the fault was the ritual, and not a fatal ignorance of organic chemistry.

This god of powerful medicine, with the proper religious rite, could be induced to give an Indian good hunting, or success in life.

But our typical young Seminole girl that we have shown in this picture number forty-three will be young and beautiful but a few short years indeed. In fifteen more years she will be fat, coarse, and ugly. Strangely enough her Romeo will look even more like a real-life Lone Ranger. Perhaps you do not want me to tell you this bride did not escape the ill effects of bad medicine for a decade. She died several years after her marriage.

Before we leave our visit with these three families who lived in the eastern part of Hendry and Collier counties I should say that there is a road to this Indian country from Clewiston which is neither more impassable nor longer. They can be reached just as readily from this white settlement and they can be induced, in time, to move up this old lake shore toward Clewiston into a stock range that is good enough to support them in the cattle industry. I hoped to use these Indians as a nucleus of my southern Indian Community, and the band about the home of Billie Stewart as the nucleus of the northern Indian Community, with the Agency at the midpoint between the two. This is good policy from the standpoint of the Indian Service, the white commonwealth of Florida, and this pathetic remnant of the proudest and most heroic of all the Indian tribes.

We have talked at length about our own difficulty with transportation through the Florida Everglades, but we have not told you much of the story of how the Indian travels. Picture number forty-four was taken at one of those eastern Collier county camps and shows a cypress canoe in dry dock. Billy Fewl is said to have rowed one of these to Havana, Cuba, but for the most part they did not get out in the open waters of the Gulf or the Atlantic. But they did steal both rapidly and silently through this large glades in these dugouts.

Photograph number forty-five is another canoe; this one is being poled along a canal by Charlie Cypress. Since the water is shallow it was better to push the dugout by a cypress pole. Photograph number forty-six is one of the more beautiful pictures of these "Indian in a canoe." It has been a popular picture, but it has never satisfied my own sense of good composition. Perhaps an artist might explain just why it so fails.

Of course these canoes were used for visiting other families, or a trip to the white markets, for hunting expeditions, and for freighting supplies both to and away from home. The Indian women and children were at home in them. Usually when I put a foot in them they had an evil way of turning over.

44

45

46

The Florida Indian did a great deal of walking. Their skill in finding their way through this region is no great marvel. They had done this from childhood, and knew both this region like a book, and what to look for in the discovery of a trail. The most sensational story that I have about this trail finding is about a group of our Indian boys at the Agency. Mr. L. B. Yates, one of our most faithful workmen, and I had returned from Immokalee with some of these native wild cows. My home was on the cattle ranges of the Panhandle of Texas, and I was certain that I could handle these Florida cows. But one got away from us when we were branding them, and she would not let us get in sight of her. I hunted for her all morning and during about half the afternoon. One of the Indians hunted me down and said that they had the cow. I said, "You mean you have found her?" He said, "No, we've got her. Josie, he catch her." Josie was the driver of my heavy tractor. I knew the Indians did not have a rope and were afoot. It was hard to believe that they had captured this wild animal. When I found Josie, his big shirt was torn and he had the mark of a cow's horn around his chest, but the cow had both of her feet tied with two neckerchieves and was too stunned to even get up when we let her loose. The Indians had not looked for her at all, but they had spent several hours looking for her tracks, and had ambushed her. Josie had overpowered her by grabbing her by the horns as she charged him. I had seen a six-foot alligator that he had captured with his bare hands, but I did not think that he knew much about cattle.

But just as the hand sewing machine, the phonograph, and the grist mill had invaded these homes, so also the model-T had become the possession of almost every family. As automobiles go they could get more out of less than any people in America. Picture number forty-seven is a typical scene. This old wreck is loaded with groceries until the springs are beating the axles. For all that is left of it, and for the awful country it must travel, it is a modern miracle. They went through swamps that I could never get my car through. If the jack was missing or they had left it at camp, one of them would lift a wheel and another would block it up with cypress logs.

I have said that Collier County had more Seminoles in it than all other counties of Florida. Not all of them lived in the Billy Fewl neighborhood. Photograph number forty-eight shows an assembly of quite a few of the Indians of this country. The Tamiami Trail had been completed and the event was celebrated by a fair. These Indians had been urged to join with several thousand whites in this festival.

Picture number forty-nine was taken at Turner's River on the Tamiami Trail. One of Chokoloskee's "Devil's angels" had moved up this river to the highway, and ran a "low bush lightning" market. Here, too, was an Indian camping ground. My interest in this picture is found in this circle of men, both eating and "chewing the rag," as we sometimes say. This is not a "barber shop quartet," but it is very definitely a stag party, and these men are enjoying this "talk, talk, talk" which they are not supposed to like.

In about 1928 this group of Indians were "struck with low bush lightning" and got into a fight. Josie Billie, one of the most hopeful of all the younger Indians of this county, was attacked and lashed back at one

48

49

of the men with a knife. A woman inter-
vened, as they so often did, and was cut with
the knife. This Devil's angel was afraid to
take her to Everglades, but started to Miami
with her for treatment. She bled to death. I
visited the place a few days later, met and
talked to Old Charlie Tigertail, and also saw
these young warriors stalking the woods with
high-powered rifles in this life and death
game of wits in which one hides and many
hunt. Josie did succeed in keeping out of
their way, and was acquitted at the Green
Corn Dance.

Photograph number fifty is a poor picture
of Charlie Tigertail. As I have said, he was
one of the direct descendents of one of the
great chiefs of the Seminoles. Although he
was too friendly with "fire water," he had a
sense of leadership and a wisdom in his notion of policy that made me admire him.
That he was generous toward a people
against whom we would be bitter if we were
in his place, shows a broadness of character
and tolerance of which the world is greatly in
need.

The next three pictures, numbers fifty-
one, fifty-two, and fifty-three, show some of

50

51

the changes in this Indian homeland that have been brought about by the development of white communities. The first is a poor picture of a sawmill that was located near the four sections tract that we set up for purchase for the Indians, and that Dr. Hartmann and I had appraised twice. This is near the distillery that Jessie Morgan, Johnny and Jim visited at the time of the death of Jessie. In setting up a telephone line between Everglades and Immokalee the Indians were employed to cut the way through the Big Cypress section. It was adjacent to this lumber mill. I have heard the foreman of this crew say that the water in this swamp was covered with water moccasins like leaves on the bed of a forest. Back in the time when our country had sent an armed force into this region to capture *all* of these people, a village was discovered by our soldiers near this spot. The mosquitoes were almost unbearable. How these soldiers ever endured such an expedition I do not know.

Numbers fifty-two and fifty-three show a very small result of a hurricane. The water has gone over this town of Everglades to a depth of six feet. These catastrophes have a way of exposing the stuff a man is made of. Judged by such standards the Indian is a tower of strength. He knows both how to conduct himself and to defend his people. He can guess the coming of a "big blow," but he will take the word of a radio a lot quicker than he will his own guesses.

In the earlier days many of the Indians who lived on this west shore line of the old Lake Okeechobee poled their canoes from Guava Camp to the east coast. The high land on which the Agency was located was a general camping ground for the whole group. A few miles to the north were the Stranahans, another great pioneer family who had the same kind of courage and character that had made the best of the Seminoles truly great. It was Kipling who said, "When two strong men stand face to face, though they come from the ends of the earth, there is neither east nor west, border, nor breed, nor birth." If ever two people represented this kind of strength within our own race they were Mr. and Mrs. Frank Stranahan.[30] Here the Seminoles sought the same wise counsel, forbearance, and high policy that they formerly had received from the greatest of their own

---

30. Frank Stranahan, a native of Ohio, established an Indian trading post on the New River in 1893. This venture prospered and he became a leading figure in the political and business life of the community which was to become Fort Lauderdale. In 1900 he married a young school teacher, Ivy Cromartie, and they soon moved into a large home on the riverfront. The Stranahans remained loyal to their Indian friends long after the trading era passed, and led the efforts to secure federal lands and services for the Seminoles. Mrs. Stranahan was particularly effective in this work through her role as Indian Chairman of the State Federation of Women's Clubs, and her friendship with various state and national political figures. At the time of her death in 1971 she was acknowledged as the major force in founding Indian aid societies in Florida. Kersey and Kushin, "Ivy Stranahan and the 'Friends of the Seminoles'," pp. 6–11; McGoun, *A Biographic History of Broward County,* pp. 58–60.

leaders. That the general public has too frequently traded such sterling virtue for the petty ethics of such a tenet as "thou shall not play mumble peg" is enough to embitter the heart and soul, unless one has that kind of virtue himself. Florida would do well to build a second Bok Tower[31] to the memory of a very great common citizen, Mrs. Frank Stranahan, who is still both wise and diligent in behalf of the needy.

Old Annie Tommie, whom I have mentioned before, gained a very great deal of her character from her association with this family. The Broward county Indians who lived as neighbors to the Stranahans have adjusted

vvvvvvvvvvvvvvvvvvvvvvvvvvvvvvvvvvvv

31. Bok Tower is a gothic-style carillon tower located in a bird sanctuary at Lake Wales, Florida. The tower was built around 1925 by Edward W. Bok, foreign-born editor of the *Ladies' Home Journal,* and donated as a gift to the American people. The tower and sanctuary were dedicated by President Hoover in 1929, and Bok was later buried on the grounds. *The National Cyclopaedia of American Biography,* vol. 13, p. 41.

themselves to the changing world about them more wisely than any other group in the state.

But the final chapter of this story is distressing rather than hopeful. As everyone knows, Miami is one of the "wide open" playgrounds of America. The *Life Magazine* recently featured some of the evils of such a city under the title of "The Miami Spectacle." Artificiality and exhibitionism are sold over the counter of commercialism in the amount of several millions of dollars per year. To cash in on the curiosity of the tourist sucker has become at least one of the aims of this industry.

I was returning from a trip to Tallahassee, and when I drove up to a filling station in Tampa for gasoline a wild-looking old man begged me to give him a ride to Sarasota. He was as hairy as a gorilla. The shaggy, coarse, half-gray and half-sun-bleached mane of his head was uncombed and hung in tangles to his shoulders. The coarse bristles of his arms and legs had more the appearance of wire than human hair. One shuddered at the thought of touching his sun-baked and scaly

hide. He had no hat nor shoes. He wore the shortest of shorts and a sleeveless and open-breasted shirt. The general scheme back of his dress was to expose every possible feature of repulsiveness.

As I looked carefully into his face I saw a rather pathetic old man who was playing a role that he did not enjoy at all. I invited him to get in my car and headed it over the first section of the famous Tamiami Trail. He unburdened his soul with a defiant, "I'm no freak." I learned that it was his act to play the freak in the Ringling Circus, and to thereby humbug the public into believing that he was some wild and impossible human being from God knows where.

The Seminoles of Dade county and along the Tamiami Trail have, without their understanding of the role they must play, been incorporated into the kind of farce that my old friend of the shaggy mane was enacting. I submit that life is not a farce to men of sterling virtue, and this kind of living degenerates the heirs of the heritage which that strong man, Osceola, gave these heroic people.

52

53

Photograph number fifty-four is a reproduction of a combination road house and Indian show place in Miami. A number of years ago Willie Willie, a Seminole, built a palm-thatched wall about his own home and proposed to open it to public gaze for an admission fee. In Florida people gather almost from the ends of the earth for relaxation. Their fagged and jaded interests in life were excited by this exhibition of a human family that was so different from anything they had ever seen. The business prospered, and Willie Willie moved to Miami and established Musa Isle, one of the most famous of these places where a human family may be pawed over, gazed at, and made the butt of rude and coarse humor. This "attraction" came, in time, to bring in a gross of $50,000 per year. Willie Willie, during his ownership of it, had more money than he could use. He married outside of his tribe and burned up the highways with his high-priced car.

In the meantime [a white man] who, according to the records of J. Edgar Hoover, had recently become an escaped convict, returned to the Miami area, "got in" with Willie Willie, and managed to get a title to Musa Isle, and dispossessed the Indian. Of all my pictures, I think, number fifty-five burns more deeply into a just-minded man than any. Willie Willie, who founded a fifty-thousand-dollar industry, died a pauper in this miserable white man's hovel. Compare this with photograph number six, and such a comparison should be made, for this is the dump the U.S. Indian Service was "good" enough to "give" him the use of after a convict had robbed him. Here he was permitted to die with tuberculosis.

This is not so much an indictment of the official who lived in the big house overlooking this wreck as it is of the whole relationship both between the government and the Indians, and the American people and these step-citizens. Although I was not that official I think sometimes, as a protest against such wrong, it would be well for the official to move out of his big house and change places with the Indian.

In the meantime [the white owner] grew in wealth and respectability. The Indians, both from Dade and Collier counties, when they came to Miami, had no place to stay but Musa Isle. He employed one or two families to act as his museum exhibits, and gave a place to sleep and a pot of stew to those not under his employment. He was permitted to order expenses for the Indians against the U.S. Indian Service. Even white citizens came to look to him to contract materials and services for the Seminoles.

The picture shown in number fifty-four is not Musa Isle, but it is another such village that [the white owner] built after we put enough heat on him to dispossess him of Willie Willie's old camp. But we might run out to this place or Musa Isle to see why it draws all of this trade. There are city buses that make the trip out there regularly, or since it is only a short distance from downtown Miami, one can drive out there in a few minutes. But this is a special day. The great circus that is Miami has given the spotlight to a water festival during the past week, and to the Hialeah Race Track the weeks before, but this one day Musa Isle has the spotlight. For some time this event has been "built up" in the press, both by advertising and by special feature stories. Its highlight will be an Indian wedding. It was Gibbons who said

54

that the "Holy Roman Empire" was neither holy, Roman, nor an empire. This is neither Indian nor a wedding, and the people of Miami know it, and even some of the tourists know it. One Indian boy was married so often that too many of the tourists [were able] to remember that "that's the boy they married off last year."

But the big item is the "gate take." The merchants are willing to give the "bride" a sewing machine or the groom a gun for the free advertising space they get from it. So the contracting parties are to be "showered" with gifts from this great white community.

If we go early we may see one of the usual "features" that are put on about every two hours per day through the tourist season. The wedding will cost extra, but the regular show is fifty cents admission. A young girl, perhaps, collects the fare, and we are allowed to go into about a block of land enclosed with a high palm-leaf-thatched wall. A few items of Indian handwork from other tribes are on display in the little shop through which one enters this arena. Inside we see, perhaps, a half dozen Seminole huts and several Indian families, either sitting on the edge of the

platforms of the house or laying on them. Some one of the women will be sitting cross-legged on one with her machine in front of her making clothes for her family. A man may be working on some toy canoe with a pocket knife or just talking with his people. The tourists will talk both loudly and freely about the damn funny clothes and the damn dirty pots, and some brute will grab the blouse of an Indian wife and yell, "Hey, Bill—Want a squaw?" The husband of the wife will see what damn fools these tourists are, but will ignore it.

But the interest of the tourist soon lags, and the show management knows this and has prepared for it. Flanked on every side of the Indian families is row after row of rattlesnakes, king snakes, and just snakes, monkeys, owls, wildcats, and the "wild and sensational creatures of the jungle." At one end of the arena is a filthy bog of double B.O.'ed alligators and crocodiles. At first "just looking" at these keeps the interest of the tourist at somewhere between just warm and white hot, but when this lags, the "barker" begins his harangue about this marvelous feat of an Indian wrestling with an alligator.

Now the 'gator is a "honey" for this kind of exploitation. He can kill a man with one powerful grip of his enormous mouth, but so will a tractor, machine gun, or a number of other machines if one does not know how to handle them. The 'gator is the nearest approach to a machine that was ever made from protoplasm. The Indian does know how to handle him without too great risk.

But in this pit of 'gators is one that is blind in one eye and has been "plowed around" until it does not care whether it is on its feet or back. After the excited tourists have gathered around the pit the barker does his best by way of harangue to make them believe that they are about to see the world's most sensational drama. His story about the Indian risking his arm or his leg always made me furious, because, first, the arm or leg are worth too much to throw away for a white man's gate take; and second, the U.S. Indian Service and not the showman pays the bill for treatment of such injury. But when words fail to keep the excitement going, an Indian boy will slip into the pool, get on the blind side of the old gator, grab him by the nose, and turn him over on his back. The show is

55

over and the crowd must get out for the next.

But this is just routine. The big event of the year will come in the afternoon. Since the Indian girl is most attractive between the ages of fifteen and twenty, the "bride" must be taken from this age group; but the Indian boy is still in the gosling stage until after he is twenty, so the "groom" must be considerably older. He often is a man with a wife and several children, but he is at his prime and is supposed to know enough acting to play this farce through to the end.

But you recall that a real Indian wedding is utterly devoid of pageantry. The best showman in the world could not merely walk a man into a camp and sell that to the tourists as a sensation. Neither can the ritual be identical with the usual "Here comes the bride." But it must be enough like the usual "thing" to convince the tourist that he has actually seen a wedding. So the show management invents the best he can think up, and the Indians rehearse the thing so they will know "just how an Indian gets married."

As the time draws near, the buses from downtown pour out excited and strange peo-ple from every part of the nation, and from every social strata of life. The stage has been well set; the show is already going strong. The cash register sings its wildest sym-phony. The packed throngs wait in eagerness for the curtain to rise, only there is no cur-tain. The "medicine man," who here is act-ing, leads these riotously dressed Indian man and girl before the crowd. In the name of matrimony he invokes a solemn pledge from each, only the girl may be giggling in the meantime. And then to ascend to the seventh heaven or pure, undiluted farce the "groom" wraps his arm about the "bride" and plants a pair of saliva-coated lips on her face. They both shudder, and she grabs her dress or cape and wipes away the residue of this filthy habit. The gifts from the stores of Miami are handed over to the "new bride and groom," and for days the Indians chuckle over what fools these tourists really are. They also wonder about that something man has called *fraud*. The more thoughtful say, "May be so alright for white man, no good for Indian."

Photograph number fifty-six was taken in-side this show place after the crowds were away. The place is clean. It has to be. These little children appeal to any average normal man. Here they learn English and a number of social conventions that are more advanced than those of their own race. But what is the children "across the railroad tracks" of any race? Is it possible to throw children into Coney Island, and rear them there, and make good citizens of them? "Street waif" is the term given to a child reared with a street for a home. The only home some of these chil-dren have is this cynosure of exhibition and sensation.

56

Photograph number fifty-seven shows the ill effects of this whole affair. It is a long, long way, not in miles but in well being, from the home of Billie Stewart or the home of Billie Fewl to the situation of the family shown here. The camp is located on the canal bank of the Tamiami Trail, about fifteen or twenty miles from Miami. They have set up their own version of Musa Isle. The tourists stop to visit with them, and they ask for money for the right to be looked at and the right to look at the little they have here. The children yell, "Nickle, nickle" and stretch out a hand to every white visitor.

Miami and Ringling Brothers know their showmanship, but what do these people know about this industry? Their camp site is squalid and becomes even more revolting. If they cage a wildcat or keep an alligator, they offend their customers by neglecting their animals. Their income is almost negligible. They take garfish from the canal, cook it whole, and sit about their tables, pull away the flesh from the intestines of the fish, and eat the flesh while the tourists look on and shudder. The hell raisers blast the Indian Agent for "letting" the Indians have such habits, and rush to the defense of the industry of Miami. The Indians wonder why the white man eats oysters "guts and all" or stands around their family table and finds fault with the way they eat, but claims to have good manners.

Picture number fifty-seven shows the poorest of the several such camps along the Tamiami Trail. But the Dade County Indians and now many of the Collier County Indians are going the way of this family. A nationally known Indian entitled her book *Indians are People Too.* So was my shaggy-haired "wild man" from Ringling's Circus, but he had done his best to make the public think he was not, and he suffered because of it. What kind of role do the Indians want to play in their relation to the other citizens of America? You can bet your last dime that Osceola, the great Seminole, could answer that. No step-citizenship for him! No "nigger" with his head through a sheet for the white crowds to throw baseballs at.

This abuse was more extensive than the city of Miami. There were exhibitions and fairs throughout the nation that drew some of Florida's Indian population to their side-shows. Some white man would get a group of Seminoles to go with him, and would give them transportation to the Chicago Fair, or other such exposition. If he got enough money out of it he would bring the Indians home. But if his business venture did not pay out he would desert them, and the U.S. Indian Service had to take over and finance enough of the venture to get the Indians back to Florida. I resented this kind of injustice to the government.

To lead these people away from this professional freakism, and the vice and crime of our cities, and to provide them with a community of their own, a community that is backed by enough income to give them a better standard of living, seems to me to be the challenge of the U.S. Indian Service of Florida. This makes that sale of $30,000 worth of Indian livestock last winter so very important, both to the Indian and to the people of Florida. These neighbors of ours don't have to lose that splendid pride that has

57

meant so much to them during their heroic past. They don't have to go to Miami, or any other city, and live in a white man's cow lot where the food is thrown to them, much as a West Texas ranchman throws hay and corn to his animals. They can develop their own leadership, and they might develop some traits of human virtue that the white man would do well to emulate.

The most dangerous of all my work with the Seminoles was done by my Special Officer, Walter B. Lewis. The Everglades region has been a part of the United States for many years, but the task of establishing law and order in parts of it has not yet been done. What might be called a kind of chamber of commerce slogan at Immokalee was that no law enforcement officer had ever been permitted to live in that village. Notwithstanding this, if we had "pulled the raw things" in Chokoloskee that we "pulled" in Immokalee we might have been mobbed. You see I had some friends both in Immokalee and the county organization who protected me and my helper. And what were the "raw things we pulled?" We got white people in trouble over Indians!

Photograph number fifty-eight shows myself, Mr. Lewis, and a group of witnesses we had taken to a federal court. Nash in his report had estimated that about sixty percent of the income of the tribe was invested in "low bush lightning." He recommended that a federal officer be assigned to Florida for a few months to break this situation up. I do not think the Indian Office could have found a better man for the work than Walter B. Lewis. But he came to Florida with authority to travel in street cars, buses, or on the railroad. I wonder what super modern train the American soldiers rode when they were scouting through the Everglades for Osceola and his band! Or what "Dixie Flyer" took our recent soldiers through the jungles of the South Sea Islands! I bought Mr. Lewis a model-A with my own personal funds, and discovered that I had to do all the repair work on it, even though I gave the government the use of it.

For my part, men can have whatever convictions they want to have about "fair play" with these "Satan Angels," but I know they will treat you about as "square" as the Japs treated their enemies. That whiskey will destroy any people is a well-known fact. One can give scores of examples of the waste and cost of this evil. Two of the young men at the Agency came up to the office one noon and wanted to be paid off for their work. They said they needed some food. I gave each his check, but said, "If you boys get drunk on that the devil will be to pay." In about two or three hours my telephone rang, and I was told that one of these boys and two Indian women were in the hospital at Ft. Lauderdale. I drove over, and the boy "beat it" because he knew I would be mad at him. The two women were in a serious condition. They had gotten drunk as soon as they could get to a bootlegger, and had wrecked their automobile. The girls stayed in the hospital for several weeks, and ran up a bill of five or six hundred dollars. An Indian Service officer does not have money unlimited. He does have to plan carefully to provide for unavoidable illness. It is not fair to the government for an Indian, or anyone else, to get relief employment, use the money to get drunk, and then run the government into five

58

hundred dollars worth of expense over his drunkenness.

One can go through the files of the Miami papers and read case after case of Indian deaths that resulted from whiskey. This also leads to every other vice. Social diseases showed a marked increase following a Green Corn Dance, because everyone got drunk.

For the Indian Service to set up law and order not only among the Indians, but in frontier white communities, is something that cannot be done in a "few months." I have at hand a report on Mr. Lewis' work that shows that he had developed seven cases at Okeechobee, four at Ft. Lauderdale, one at Ft. Pierce, six at Arcadia, two at Immokalee, five at Ft. Myers, seven at Miami, and seven at other points, or a total of thirty-nine cases. He got sixteen convictions out of this. It is almost unbelievable the amount of work involved in these cases. He had to make two purchases of whiskey from each bootlegger, after which he made the charge before a U.S. Commissioner, got the Indian witnesses to the federal grand jury which met at Miami, Tampa, or Jacksonville, and finally got these same Indians before the court at the appointed hour of the trial. In this picture are ten Seminoles. They come from places that are a hundred miles apart. They hunt, trap, or roam the Everglades day by day. To find them when the court wanted them was not a street car job. If the witness did not appear, the case was lost.

On one of these trips when Lewis had to find his men and get them together for a trip to Jacksonville he rounded up a number of them back near Guava Camp, and since he had more than he could bring out with his car, he got one of the Indians to bring his car. But the Indian car ran out of gas, and Lewis tied it behind his and was pulling both cars loaded with men out of the Everglades. Of course he soon had his engine hot, and he stopped back in the swamp at a white hut to get water. This man had gotten back away from everybody, because he hoped to get away from all law enforcement. About a year before this Lewis had convicted him on a charge of selling whiskey to the Indians, and he had just returned from the penitentiary.

Lewis had no idea that this man lived at this hut. When he knocked a boy came to the door, and gave him a bucket of water, and Lewis went back to the car with it, and began to fill his radiator. In the meantime the bootlegger got it straightened out in his mind that that was the officer who had sent him up. He made for his shotgun, but the boy got to Lewis first and told Lewis that his dad was coming to shoot him. The Indians were frightened and scattered like quail. Lewis had a small thirty-two pistol, but he had had a lot of years of experience in outfacing the other man. He stood his ground, and told the boy that if his dad came out there that one of them would die. The dad did not come. Lewis gathered up his Indians and got them to the court on schedule. Nobody took a beating worse than these liquor law enforcement officers. I know for I knew not only the work of this man but a number of them out of Miami. One of the most admirable young men I ever met was the Indian Office administrator of this program. J. Edgar Hoover never had a cleaner or more efficient officer in the whole FBI organization. I met him after the new brass hats in Washington had kicked out Lewis and my own set-up was running madly at cross-purposes. He had been outmoded, too, by the New Deal. But no one will ever alter the chemical reaction of a liquor-soaked human mind. Collier may have stopped the Indian liquor law enforcement, but he did not stop the toll of death that grows out of this evil.

Lewis was the only man I had to help me out in the field. I needed him, not only to trap bootleggers, but to enforce the whole body of law in behalf of the Seminoles. I kept him when I got him after a lot of "justification" before the Washington office. Collier notwithstanding, he was greatly needed in the Florida work. In time the people of south Florida would have come to know that it was a violation of law to sell or give whiskey to their Indian neighbors, and he might have aided in establishing law and order in some of these more frontier communities.

The primary issue between John Collier and me was neither Lewis nor this recourse to law to establish temperance. He is basically and fundamentally a pagan—a lover of life in the raw. He romanticizes and idealizes the primitive and jungle life. He would exterminate progress and throw "its whole blooming works out." The days of the tepee, the tomahawk, war paint and war bonnets belonged to the childhood of the Indian race. If they want to be "people too," they have got to play a different role in this mighty commonwealth.

This government by and through circumvention of legal authority is a most vicious crime in Russia or Germany. But the ward boss politician has always influenced government policy and action in America, and has always gotten a place on the government payroll where he could circumvent those in authority. A missionary said to me, "We are the only officials in the state. You let me have the government funds that go to my three-fourths of the Seminoles, and you can have what goes to your one-fourth." When I visited another jurisdiction the officer in charge said, "You see that school teacher. She has everybody at this unit under her thumb. Whatever she says goes with Washington." The Lord help a field administrator when the departments within his bureau at Washington begin open warfare between themselves. Health promotes his field nurse or doctor over and above anything the officer in charge proposes. Education promotes its field teaching staff over and above his recommendations. There is the contemptible practice of dropping "official" correspondence, and sending "personal" mail to the headquarters. The administrator must see the official mail of his staff, but a nurse or teacher can write personal letters to the head nurse or head instructor, and he knows nothing about it.

And there is this method of establishing facts by fiat. The big bull that can bellow the most emphatically, and can reinforce his bellow with profanity, is right. I said to my nurse, "I saw the child yesterday and the doctor had visited him." She said, "No, he did not. Of course he didn't. Now you see he didn't." That was something new to me. I had never seen facts "made" that way before. But her medical staff in Washington would make that the "official fact" in the whole bureau of Indian Affairs. This is an easy way to grab "success"—just claim it by fiat. It is also an effective way toward this circumvention of authority. One of the governors of Texas said, "If Texas goes to hell under my administration it will go by law." The government in recent years has swung strongly to the other extreme. It is the best way to make a monkey out of this whole business of government authority.

I had the old-fashioned notion that one's work was more important than one's rank, station or wealth. Scattergood said to me in Washington in 1931, "We want to establish a willingness for service among Indian Service employees."[32] To serve the government, to get its work done, seems to me to be the first consideration. I learned that there was a feu-

dal system in government circles, and that the big house you lived in, the high sounding title, and the salary you drew were impressive items in the capitol of a great democracy. *Government* employees were just too mighty to live in the field of their work. A big city was the only dignified environment worthy of their station. The medical staff "burned me up" for recommending that their nurse ought to live near her work. It is not surprising that the new administration that followed me required the Seminoles to enter the office of their Agency by the back door.

One of the most marvelous men in all of American history was "big chief Osceola," as the Seminoles call him. He was superb, magnificent, and all the other adjectives one

can add. He rises above the swamps of the Everglades like a "looming mystery," a "tower of strength," a "flame of righteous passion." There was a wideness in his character, a nobleness in his will and action that made [Gen. Thomas G.] Jesup, his adversary, seem mean and small. When Jesup took him prisoner under a pretense of negotiating a peace between the Seminoles and the United States, and threw him in the old dungeon at St. Augustine, he refused to "escape" like a criminal, but said, "My captors threw me in by the front door. I shall wait until they lead me out by the front door." There are times when it is more important to remain in jail or die than to roam a hillside and live, as a few "Quislings" of this day are discovering. When that most fundamental of human virtue is gone, the end of human life is not distant. Florida ought to have a couple of Bok Towers built in memory of this matchless hero.

In photograph number fifty-nine I give you Osceola, the defiant leader of a proud people.

In many respects it is a long road between

---

32. J. Henry Scattergood, the Quaker treasurer of Bryn Mawr College and a member of the Indian Rights Association, was appointed Assistant Commissioner of Indian Affairs in 1929. Serving with his friend, Commissioner C.J. Rhoads (see note 3 above), they formed an effective team to begin the reform of federal Indian policy. Much of their initial effort was carried forward and implemented during the New Deal era, but Scattergood and Rhoads both left the Indian Service in 1933 at the beginning of the new Roosevelt administration. Tyler, *A History of Indian Policy*, pp. 116–18.

59

60

Osceola and Billie Stewart, who is pictured in this next photograph, number sixty. But this road is not all down grade. Billie Stewart was a good neighbor, a wise and tolerant man, a good husband and father, and one of the best American citizens among the Seminoles.

It is foolish for any kind of "up lifter" to try to tell people what they shall wear. This is one of Linn's pictures. I never saw Billie Stewart with this kind of costume on, but it, at least, shows a willingness to strike out on the new road to that land where "Indians are people too," where the tepee, the tomahawk, war paint, and life by warfare are left behind. And it is my guess that he would be happy to be joined in this journey by his white neighbors.

James Lafayette Glenn